Olmsted's Riverside

Olmsted's RIVERSIDE

Stewardship Meets Innovation in a Landmark Village

CATHY JEAN MALONEY

SOUTHERN ILLINOIS UNIVERSITY PRESS & CARBONDALE

Southern Illinois University Press
www.siupress.com

First printed October 2024.

Front cover and title page illustration: Rebuilt water tower. Chris Neumer
and Twenty Seven and a Half Photography. *Back cover illustrations, top to
bottom*: Gas lamps in Riverside, an American Elm in Guthrie Park,
and native plantings and climate-appropriate cultivars in the village.
Photos by author.

ISBN 978-0-8093-3952-5 (paperback)
ISBN 978-0-8093-3953-2 (ebook)
This book has been catalogued with the Library of Congress.

Printed on recycled paper

SIU
Southern Illinois University System

For the quiet people in Riverside, who sought
neither fame nor fortune but who
Planted a native tree
Picked up a piece of litter
Photographed a bird and shared with others
Volunteered for a project
Added to, defended, researched, or simply enjoyed
the beauty and importance of Riverside—
Your work is well noted and appreciated.

CONTENTS

ACKNOWLEDGMENTS

Writing a historical book, even in the Internet age, requires rumbling around in dusty archives and connecting with curators of same. I am indebted to archivists and librarians especially from the Chicago History Museum, Chicago Public Library, Newberry Library, Library of Congress, Riverside Public Library, and Riverside Historical Museum.

Early readers of my manuscript saved me from many an embarrassing misstatement of fact. They include Constance Guardi and Jim Petrzilka from the Riverside Historical Museum; Malcolm Cairns, professor emeritus, Ball State University landscape architecture department; and Scott Mehaffey, executive director at Farnsworth House National Historic Site. Any remaining errors in the book are mine.

Local photographers in Riverside have graciously allowed me to use their pictures. These creative individuals include William Suriano, Chris Neumer, and Valerie Jisa. Just one of their beautiful images is well worth a thousand of my words.

The editors and staff at Southern Illinois University Press have been a delight. They are at once nimble yet exacting, encouraging, and pragmatic. I have thoroughly enjoyed working with them.

Husband Mike shares with me a love for Riverside and a love of reading. I also share with him all my troubles and countless frustrations with footnotes. Thank you, Mike.

Olmsted's Riverside

The rebuilt water tower overlooks Riverside's abundant greenery. The water tower was one of Olmsted's "artificial improvements" to bring the luxuries of the city to the rural suburb. Photo by Twenty Seven and a Half Photography.

Introduction

While on the phone with a landscape architect recently, I mentioned where I lived. "Riverside," he mused. "That's an interesting artifact."

Artifact? Like a vestigial tail or a buggy whip? Something past its prime that belongs in a curiosity cabinet? To me, a Riverside resident of more than 30 years, the thriving, beautiful 150-plus-year-old community glows with health and promise. This model suburb created by Frederick Law Olmsted and Calvert Vaux in 1869 inspires today's urban planners, landscape architects, and community designers. Equally important, Riverside's long stewardship tradition to safeguard and invigorate this national treasure offers lessons to any community.

This is not just local boosterism. Olmsted's design for Riverside, Illinois, has outlasted technology changes, environmental disruption, demographic shifts, and tugs-of-war between public and private property rights. The Riverside General Plan of 1869 successfully pioneered subsequent master planning models and included walkability, integrated green space, mixed housing stock, transit-oriented development, sense of community, quality architecture, and more elements to enhance quality of life. If everything old is new again, Riverside is the ultimate urban planning blueprint.

Olmsted and Vaux created Riverside, just outside of Chicago, at the behest of real estate investors.[1] The plan incorporated the best ideas about working with nature to enhance residents' overall well-being. Olmsted's social reform philosophies, including democratic ideals, healthful living, and moral inspiration, underpinned the design. While pioneering, the design reflected the cumulative ideals of leading authors, reformers, and community planners of the day and of the years before. Still, Riverside was not created as a utopia but as a profitable investment. Having seen the success of New York's Central Park and other green spaces in raising nearby property values, Riverside's investors hoped for sensational sales of their master-planned village fitted with an abundance of greenery.

The Riverside plan boldly broke from previous grid-based city plans. The effect on the psyche is subtle: gently curved roads offer soothing vistas of abundant greenery and of the village's namesake, the Des Plaines River. According to Olmsted scholar Charles Beveridge, "As a result of [Olmsted's] own experience and wide reading, he concluded that the most powerful effect of scenery was one that worked by an unconscious process."[2] Now a National Historic Landmark village, Riverside's classic design still evokes this intuitive embrace.

Scholarly articles and books routinely hail Riverside as a milestone in suburban planning but then abruptly leave the story of the village in 1869. With so many traits of a desirable town plan, is it not worthwhile to examine how these features might be translated to other American communities? And, to learn how the design survived more or less intact, should we not consider the threats and opportunities posed to the plan in the past fifteen decades? This book attempts to answer both of these questions. While I briefly mention the architecture in the village, there are other books that extol Riverside buildings by Frank Lloyd Wright, William Le Baron Jenney, Louis Sullivan, and other luminaries. My main emphasis is on the more fragile and ephemeral elements of the cultural landscape—the green spaces—and how their usage changes over time.

Although Frederick Law Olmsted had already earned a reputation as a preeminent designer while planning Riverside, it was not until about 100 years later that serious scholarship on his work began with the Olmsted Papers Project in 1972. Two years prior, the National Park Service had designated Riverside as a National Historic Landmark. Thus, not only had a century passed before Riverside received any preservation status, but in the 50-plus years since, a host of new challenges has confronted the residents. The lessons from Riverside's success and setbacks in stewardship over the decades will be useful to town planners and residents of any cherished community.

The push-pull of progress versus preservation plays out in several arenas. There are questions about how the role of commerce (Riverside's modest central business district) might potentially compete with residential interests. Other persistent issues over the years have included differences in active or passive recreational use of green space, use of native or nonnative plantings, extent of outdoor signage, landscaping standards, use of quasi-public space, light pollution, noise abatement, river pollution and flooding, zoning issues, federal and state regulations, and, more recently, the impact of climate change. Multigenerational residents know what has historically been done, new residents ask what else can be done, and everyone has the age-old, imponderable question, "What would Olmsted do?"

"What would Olmsted do?," a rhetorical query literally posed by modern-day residents, aims to imbue Olmsted's philosophical ideals into any major decision affecting the village's design. The goal is not necessarily to slavishly replicate the materials and exact elements of his plan into a world that, in more than 150 years, has changed. Rather, it is to understand his thinking and, where possible, preserve for residents and visitors alike the thoughtful, naturalistic landscape design. To everyone's bedevilment, Olmsted left no detailed planting plans for the village. Some residents have argued that, as a progressive thinker, Olmsted would adopt the latest technology or planting philosophy of today. There is appeal to this line of thought, until one considers that nearly all of America's luminaries were also progressive thinkers. Does this give the stewards of historic landmarks carte blanche to modify for today's needs? Should, for example, the Thomas Jefferson Foundation convert the historic Monticello vineyards and vegetable gardens to an eco-friendly forest suitable for the Piedmont region? As is frequently the case, progress is pitted against preservation as a false choice.

Trade-offs between environmental considerations and preservation concerns surface frequently in historic communities, including Riverside. Olmsted's signature greenswards, large expanses of smooth lawn, for example, have lately come under attack from ecologists who see turf as monocultures awash in polluting chemicals. Recently, a wonderful landscape architect prepared a plan for a small but degraded green space in Riverside. To replace the turf and trees, the landscape architect proposed a more ecologically friendly solution with an herbaceous layer of prairie plant natives. When asked whether he could modify the design to a more traditional tree and grass combination, he remarked, "Oh, you mean, Riverside as a museum." What is the correct response? Would prairie plants disrupt the overall harmony of trees and turf that tie together individual residences and public parks? Or, is it better to contribute more healthy habitats to Illinois, the "Prairie State," where only 1 percent of prairies remain?[3]

Riverside, like many areas in the American Midwest, is not immune to climate change. Heavy rainfalls throughout the Des Plaines River watershed result in floods in Riverside. Presciently, Olmsted had reserved the riverbanks for greenery—which can absorb the excess water—never residential or commercial structures. Indeed, increased flooding events in recent years prompted a landscape change to one of Riverside's most iconic vistas—the outlook over the river valley in an area called Swan Pond. Heretofore a pastoral view of greensward and trees, the Swan Pond's manicured landscape was no longer sustainable since standing floodwater killed the grass and prevented regular mowing. After consulting with a landscape architect and the village's Landscape Advisory Commission, the village staff and volunteers replaced part of the lawn in the most significant flood-prone area with wetland native plants. More recently, the entirety of Swan Pond was designated a managed natural area, with trial and error in use to gauge the effectiveness of the new habitat. Bioswales are also being introduced in other parts of Olmsted's landscape.

Author and landscape architecture professor Richard Melznick proposes that historic landscape stewards find solutions more resilient to climate change. By identifying nonnegotiable aspects of a historic landscape and allowing for potential substitutions in others, he offers a compromise. Suggesting a broader plant palette, for example, Melznick recommends "a more flexible understanding of what we mean by character-defining features, for example, especially when it comes to historic plant materials and plant communities."[4] Such is the continuum of choices that Riverside residents, and all stewards of historic landscapes, now face.

Climate change is the latest threat that dominates today's headlines, and it may be the most significant. Yet, Riverside has faced many other challenges during the past several decades that have tested the essence of Olmsted's design. Flooding and river

This view from Bourbon Springs across Swan Pond to the Des Plaines River, ca. 1888, remains one of Riverside residents' favorites. The topography of Swan Pond has changed greatly, but the pastoral scenery remains. Village of Riverside, Riverside Historical Commission.

pollution have relentlessly plagued generations of Riversiders, with different causes and solutions in each era. Riverside residents have targeted health issues, from mosquitoes to unleashed dogs, with ordinances or publicity campaigns. Debates over the optimal use of public land have caused lawsuits.

Yet, Riverside remains, very close to the original plan as laid out by Olmsted and Vaux after 150 years. The combination of stewardship and Olmsted's design genius warrants a look at Riverside for inspiration in other communities. Olmsted's Riverside is not an artifact but a living work of art, which may be appreciated for generations to come. We may never know what Olmsted would do. As stewards, we must develop basic principles to identify and preserve the true genius of place while adapting to the most pernicious of today's challenges.

This overlook onto Swan Pond and the river may have been inspired by the travels through natural scenery Olmsted once enjoyed as a youth. Photo by author.

CHAPTER I

Laying the Groundwork:
Olmsted and Community Planning

You know him, even if you can't recollect his name. Twenty-three states lay claim to his major projects—and that doesn't even count those by his sons and successor firm. It's a prestigious list: Central Park, New York City; Stanford and Yale Universities; Arnold Arboretum, Boston; Niagara Falls State Park; Yosemite; Biltmore Estate, North Carolina. These and hundreds more are the work of Frederick Law Olmsted Sr. Olmsted (1822–1903), arguably the most influential and celebrated landscape architect in the United States, has richly enhanced Americans' enjoyment of nature, whether they know it or not.

And, he'd likely be at peace with that anonymity. Olmsted's design theories included the notion that nature's beauty worked subliminally, or "unconsciously," as he and other contemporary philosophers termed the process. His designed landscapes, holistically integrated with natural landforms and architecture, do not shout for attention but instead whisper quietly to the better angels within us. He created landscapes to fulfill democratic and social ideals, not just to ornament the grounds or architecture.

Olmsted's landscape designs offered not just pleasing natural scenery, thoughtful circulation routes, and practical infrastructure. His intent in developing plans, particularly Riverside, was to effect through his art some social good. With the right mix of plantings, design, architecture, "artificial improvements," and homes, Olmsted sought to improve humankind's civility, health, and happiness. With the social betterment goals of his designs, Olmsted brought

not only his own genius to the art of laying out grounds but also evolving theories from abroad and the United States. His personal history, coupled with contemporary movements in philosophical thinking and community development, helped make Riverside a pioneering suburban design. To understand how the man met the moment, we first look at Olmsted's biographical milestones and philosophical influences and then at the progress of community development.

FROM DABBLER TO DESIGNER

Frederick Law Olmsted (the "Law" honored an uncle's surname) was born in Hartford, Connecticut, in an era of heady philosophical exchange among local residents. Hartford was founded in 1635 by clergyman Thomas Hooker and some 100 sympatico settlers from the Massachusetts Bay Colony. This independent spirit and reverence for democracy underpinned the fabric of the Hartford community. It was the nexus of many thought leaders in social reform, democracy, and city planning.[1]

Olmsted's unorthodox education, the Hartford physical environment and intellectual milieu, and his desultory and sundry career paths as a young man improbably forged his skills as a landscape architect. In addition to his attendance at the Hartford Grammar School, Olmsted boarded with a variety of clergymen, who tutored him as a youth. From them he gained some theological concepts

Painted by his friend John Singer Sargent in 1895, this image of the elderly Olmsted is depicted walking in picturesque scenery. Courtesy of Biltmore Estate.

but also, from the more tyrannical, a distaste for strict authority. This latter aversion to dogmatic, rigid thinking may have contributed to his willingness to create iconoclastic designs.

Olmsted never formally joined a church, although he professed to be a Christian.[2] Formalized religion seemed to alienate him, as he wrote to friend Frederick Kingsbury in 1846: "I am beginning to have a horror of ministers. They are such a set of conceited, dogmatical, narrow minded, misanthropic, petty mind tyrants."[3] He preferred "a great many independent and agrarian and revolutionary ideas."[4] Nonetheless, Olmsted, like many society leaders of the day, equated Christianity with civility.

Olmsted often explored the countryside as, in today's parlance, a free-range child. Staying overnight at the homes of family and friends in nearby hamlets, he enjoyed their gardens and libraries. He and his younger brother John attended many lectures from famous intellectuals at Hartford's Young Men's Institute, absorbing the rarefied air of intellectualism.[5]

In his own recollection of youthful experiences that prepared him for his landscape career, Olmsted remembered his solo adventures in the countryside, as well as journeys with kindred spirits "more than ordinarily susceptible to beauty of scenery." He credited the readings of "[Uvedale] Price, [William] Gilpin, [William] Shenstone and [William] Marshall" for his avocation.[6] Although he was a keen observer, at age fourteen Olmsted's eyesight was unfortunately impeded by a severe case of sumac poisoning, which deterred his college enrollment. Instead, he continued his independent study and embarked on a series of short-lived careers, each of which ultimately contributed to his life's calling.

John Olmsted Sr., a prosperous merchant, bankrolled or otherwise supported the early careers of his son Frederick. Described as indulgent toward his children by Olmsted biographers, John Olmsted Sr. enjoyed a comfortable lifestyle.[7] A member of the Sons of the American Revolution, he traced his ancestry to the original Massachusetts colony. As such, his inherited landholdings and his professional contacts were substantial.

After some unsuccessful apprenticeships in his father's profession as a dry goods merchant in New York, young Frederick Olmsted decided that seafaring might be his calling. Accordingly, in the spring of 1843, at twenty-one years old, he joined the crew of the *Ronaldson* sailing from New York City to Canton, China. He endured a one-year horror of a trip, including bouts of debilitating seasickness, typhoid fever, rheumatic pains, cramped quarters, spoiled rations, and backbreaking work. Sailors who didn't pull their weight were flogged, and while Olmsted avoided this fate, he nonetheless determined after the *Ronaldson* returned to New York that seamanship was not his future.

Perhaps a land-based occupation like farming would do. He spent the next year gaining an informal education by auditing agricultural lectures at Yale, reading and consulting with farming experts. He sought a letter of introduction from farm journal publisher Luther Tucker, meeting at the same time preeminent landscape gardener Andrew Jackson Downing (1815–52). Downing, from whom Olmsted would inherit the title "Father of American Landscape Architecture" and to whom Olmsted dedicated his first book, led the chorus for public parks, domestic tranquility, and naturalistic landscape design in the United States.[8] In addition to publishing the very influential *Horticulturist* magazine, Downing wrote his first book, *A Treatise on the Theory and Practice of Landscape Gardening, Adapted to North America*, which became a textbook for American landscape design. Downing was a mentor to Olmsted, and his theories of naturalistic design heavily influenced Riverside and other Olmsted plans.

In the spring of 1846, Olmsted apprenticed at George Geddes's farm near Rochester, New York. Geddes was known for his "model

This plan of a New York "suburban villa" from Andrew Jackson Downing shows curving walkways, massed shrubbery, and rustic seating. Illustrated by Alexander Jackson Davis from *A Treatise on the Theory and Practice of Landscape Gardening, Adapted to North America*, by Andrew J. Downing, 1858. Metropolitan Museum of Art, Harris Brisbane Dick Fund, 1924. Accession Number: 24.66.361.

farm," using the latest techniques for productivity. This would mark an important foray into the emerging field of "scientific farming" for Olmsted, which also helped anchor his landscape designs in pragmatic horticultural techniques.

With his father's financial backing, Olmsted purchased a farm in Sachem's Head, Connecticut, and later another farm, Tosomock, on Staten Island. He employed drainage techniques that he had seen in Europe, laying clay tiles under farmland. In addition to planting the usual grain crops, Olmsted invested in orchard fruits such as peaches and pears. Having read Downing and other theories of design, he rearranged the grounds for artistic and functional purposes, moving outbuildings behind the residence and planting ornamental shrubs and vines near the doorway. He served with various local civic organizations and helped establish an agricultural society.[9] These experiences contributed to his pragmatic and aesthetic goals in landscaping.

Yet his peripatetic ways could not be contained. Hearing that his brother John and roommate Charles Loring Brace planned a trip to Europe, Olmsted longed for the adventure. With the plausible explanation that the trip would assist in observing the European method of scientific farming, he obtained his father's blessing, along with funding help. The young trio set sail for England for about six months of travel and adventure in the spring of 1850.

The twenty-eight-year-old Olmsted delighted in his rambles around England, noting social customs, moved by inequalities in living standards, and inspired by the city and country landscapes. Birkenhead Park, in particular, impressed him with its naturalistic design and accessibility to people of all demographics. Birkenhead, designed by preeminent landscape gardener Sir Joseph Paxton, became the first park in England funded by public monies. Observing the variety of park visitors, Olmsted noted, "And all this magnificent pleasure-ground is entirely, unreservedly, and forever the People's own. The poorest British peasant is as free to enjoy it in all its parts, as the British Queen."[10] This mingling of the masses helped prove the possibilities for democratic public grounds in America.

Olmsted also noted that the town that emerged around the park "had increased remarkably in value." Not only was it an "agreeable and healthy place of residence," but Olmsted also said that it was "the only town I ever saw that has been really built at all in accordance with the advanced science, taste, and enterprising spirit that are supposed to distinguish the nineteenth century."[11]

Returning home in the fall of 1850, Olmsted felt compelled to write about his experience. Mentor A. J. Downing published Olmsted's "The People's Park at Birkenhead" in *The Horticulturalist* in May 1851. This literary effort and others prompted Olmsted to publish his first book in 1852, *Walks and Talks of an American Farmer in England*. His foray into the literary world, courtesy of publisher and neighbor George Putnam, not only introduced Olmsted to even more prominent thinkers of the day but also launched his next career, that of journalist.

At the suggestion of friend Charles Loring Brace, the *New York Daily Times* assigned Olmsted to write a series of articles on a tour of the southern states, with particular focus on the economics of slavery and agriculture. For almost seventeen months between 1852 and 1854, Olmsted traveled from Virginia through Louisiana observing agricultural and social conditions. Another assignment brought him to Texas and the Southwest. He compiled these reports into two other books, *A Journey in the Seaboard Slave States* (1856) and *A Journey through Texas; or, A Saddle-Trip on the South-western Frontier* (1857). In the foreword to the first book, Olmsted took great pains to declare himself an impartial observer in reporting on slavery. Scholars debate whether Olmsted was an abolitionist: he certainly did not excuse the horrors of slavery, yet, according to biographer Laura Wood Roper, he likely approved of a more gradual approach toward emancipation.[12] Whereas today's definition of democratic ideals covers all races, creeds, and genders, in Olmsted's time it was less inclusive. It was unusual to propose, as he did, intermingling of different economic classes.

In 1855, Olmsted acquired a financial interest in *Putnam's Magazine*. His role included networking with some of the era's foremost writers, including William Thackeray, Washington Irving, Ralph Waldo Emerson, Henry Wadsworth Longfellow, Asa Gray, Harriet Beecher Stowe, and other contributors.[13] These literary pursuits not only offered stimulating conversations with the nation's top thinkers but also name recognition for the farmer-turned-publisher.

The real milestone in Olmsted's life, however, occurred in 1857 with a chance meeting with one of the commissioners of New York City's nascent Central Park. City planners had aspired to the park for years, with major proponents such as Downing (before his untimely death in 1852). The commissioners were seeking a park superintendent. Olmsted cobbled together salient features from his various careers for a résumé, including demonstrated agricultural success and leadership (supervising a handful of laborers at his leveraged farms) and studies of European park systems (on holiday with his friends). Additionally, he literally wrote the book on farm economics. He submitted these qualifications along with a blue-ribbon list of sponsors, including Washington Irving, Asa Gray, and William Cullen Bryant and a petition of 200 other signatures.[14]

Landing that superintendency launched Olmsted on his landscape architecture vocation. Architect Calvert Vaux, a fellow acolyte of A. J. Downing, reached out to partner with Olmsted on their winning design for Central Park. Olmsted and Vaux's 1858 successful plan, called the "Greensward Plan," included a mix of passive and active recreation areas and a unique treatment of circulation roadways using overpasses and underpasses to conceal the prosaic from the natural scenery and to separate vehicular from pedestrian traffic.

The high visibility and unparalleled success of Central Park gave Olmsted and Vaux national, even international, acclaim. The duo was hired to oversee construction of the park, which opened to the public in 1858 and soon hosted millions of visitors per year.[15] With this credential, the company of Olmsted and Vaux, and later iterations of the firm, engaged in high-profile designs for public and private clients through the remainder of the century and early into the next. It was this success that brought Olmsted to the attention of Riverside's developers.

The timing of his engagement with Central Park must have been bittersweet: Olmsted's brother John died of tuberculosis in 1857. As was often the custom, Frederick Olmsted married his brother's widow, Mary Cleveland Perkins Olmsted, in 1859, and adopted her three children (his nephews and niece). He and Mary would have two more children that survived to adulthood. (Stepson and nephew John Charles Olmsted and son Frederick Law Olmsted Jr. would ultimately work with their father and become successors to his business.) With a family to support, Frederick Sr. could no longer afford the drifting days of youth. Olmsted began his most important work to date.

PHILOSOPHICAL IDEALS

Olmsted's early life experiences, the people he met, and the trends of the day helped form the brilliance of his designs. His planned landscapes span the decades from the late 1850s to the early 1890s. Underlying each design, and constantly evolving, were some of the following principles.

Naturalistic Design

Historical, emerging, and sometimes competing styles of landscape design informed Olmsted's view of community planning. Olmsted had studied various landscape styles and personally visited different landscapes, particularly in England. Evidence of his background reading and influencers is apparent in the names he chose for Riverside roads. Of the names printed on the General Plan of Riverside, most fall into one of four categories: historical figures or events (for example, Scottswood Road), local landmarks (such as Fairbank and Bloomingbank Roads), naturalists (Audubon, Bartram, and Michaux Roads), or landscape designers and authors (Kent, Loudon, and Uvedale Roads).[16] Of the landscape designers, most hailed from England. William Kent (1685–1748), English artist and landscape gardener, popularized the English style of natural gardens. Scottish botanist and designer J. C. Loudon (1783–1843) became known for the "gardenesque" theory as well as for his argument to include greenery in cities, as written in his 1829 *Hints for Breathing Places for Metropolis*. In his 1794 *Essay on the Picturesque, as Compared with the Sublime and the Beautiful*, Sir Uvedale Price (1747–1829) favored retaining existing old growth and quaint structures in a design. Humphry Repton (1752–1818), with his 1806 *Inquiry into the Changes of Taste in Landscape Gardening, with Some Observations on Its Theory and Practice*, explored evolution of design theory and, with his famed "Red Book" overlay drawings, pioneered marketing for landscape designers. In addition to these European forerunners, Olmsted named a Riverside road after American A. J. Downing. Coupled with Calvert Vaux's *Villas and Cottages* book, a worthy template for Riverside's design emerged.

In his design for Riverside, Olmsted synthesized the best of these writings and examples. He retained existing plantings and landforms wherever possible. He employed native plants because of their hardiness but was not slavish in their use. He mixed picturesque scenes near natural features, particularly along the river, but also offered pastoral greenswards. He avoided peppering the landscape with man-made objects. His designs, for parks and other landscapes like Riverside, incarnated his reformist ideals for social good.

Domesticity

The notion of virtue blossoming from a spiritual home underpinned the Victorian value of domesticity. As the place of work became distinct from the home, with men commuting to their jobs, and a women's sphere becoming the home, so was she charged with creating a nurturing environment. Ministers glorified the virtue of a tranquil, God-centered home. As author Robert Fishman argues, Olmsted contemporaries Vaux, Downing, and Catharine Beecher Americanized the European definitions of domesticity and "preached the virtues of the detached villa in a picturesque landscaped setting as the ideal environment for American domesticity."[17]

Domesticity underwent an American spin notably from author Catharine Beecher, who opened the Hartford Female Seminary and wrote *A Treatise on Domestic Economy* (1841). In the *Preliminary Report upon the Proposed Suburban Village at Riverside, Near Chicago*, Olmsted wrote that, when designed well, suburbs attained "the most refined and soundly wholesome form of domestic life, and the best application of the arts of civilization to which man has yet attained."[18] It was a fine line between the sheltered domesticity that a home provided and the public community that Olmsted espoused. Properly designed, with setbacks from the public street and sheltered nooks in the tree-shaded grounds, a home could both be private and still contribute to the overall community landscape.[19]

Democracy

Olmsted believed his landscape efforts could be instrumental in effecting democratic ideals among Americans. Chief among these goals was inculcating a sense of community and civility; he even believed that his landscapes could act as a positive influence in shaping one's character.[20] Although today we might look askance at his development of upper-middle-class suburbs or estates for the über-wealthy, Olmsted aimed to create public spaces accessible to all. Author Scott Roulier concedes that Olmsted, as a product of his times and circumstances, may have had a class bias, but his writings about and designs for parks emphasized the commingling of all socioeconomic groups.[21] His spaces included elements for community gathering, both great and intimate. In Central Park this can be seen in the design that included (by client demand) playgrounds and a military parade, offset by quiet areas such as the Ramble, the Great Lawn, and Sheep Meadow.

Olmsted struggled with the contradiction of what he termed "exertive" versus "receptive" recreation, the former including most sports and the latter including relaxing appreciation of nature. In 1858 Olmsted wrote, "Sports, games and parades, in which comparatively few can take part, will only be admissible in cases where they may be supposed to contribute indirectly to the pleasure of a majority of those visiting the park."[22] Using massed plantings and curving paths to separate ball fields from scenic tableaux, Olmsted accomplished both aims in Central Park. In Riverside, the dual goals of community gatherings and character enhancement were evidenced through his space labeled "Picnic Island," separated by many picturesque paths for private strolling. Olmsted also enthused over the European practice of the promenade, viewing this as an opportunity to bring diverse groups together. He tried to bring the socially uplifting practice of the promenade to Riverside, intending well-built sidewalks and a beautifully designed parkway to the city, but this latter feature was ultimately never built.

Unconscious Influence

The unconscious, or involuntary awareness, of scenery was central to Olmsted's design. The unconscious would beckon a viewer to enter a contemplative state, as part of a learning process, receptive to nature's beauties.[23] Positive moral character could also be transmitted, unconsciously, from exposure to nature and others' affirming character. It was a philosophical idea, notably brought forth by New Haven theologian Horace Bushnell in the 1840s. In a brief sermon, Bushnell emphasized how humankind could influence positive social good by unpublicized example. He also drew a comparison from the natural world: "Behind the mere show, the out-ward noise and stir of the world, nature always conceals her hand of control, and the laws by which she rules."[24]

As part of the unconscious influence in Riverside, Olmsted ensured that no plantings stood out and clamored for attention. Man-made objects were limited in the spaces dedicated to natural scenes. Homes, necessary for human domestication, were shrouded by trees. With these design techniques, the beauty of nature would gently imbue residents with its charms.

Social Reform

Mid-nineteenth-century New England nurtured a culture of social reform, exposing Olmsted to readings and discussions of a broad range of ideas. His good friend and Yale confidant Charles Loring Brace founded the Children's Aid Society and supported, for better or worse, the Orphan Train movement. Friend, author, and Boston minister Edward Everett Hale espoused better education, abolition of slavery, and religious tolerance. Olmsted's hometown of Hartford nurtured a stellar cast of reform-minded leaders. As urban planner and scholar Donald Poland writes, "The ideals of natural scenery, picturesque landscape design, taste, character, domesticity and civilizing society coalesced in Hartford during Olmsted's formative years in Hartford."[25] Not only could immersion in nature soothe the soul, but it could improve one's moral character.[26]

Public Health

As cities grew, overcrowding and poor sanitary systems created a fertile ground for communicable diseases. The nineteenth century has been dubbed by some scholars "the great sanitary awakening."[27] In the 1840s, following a series of cholera, typhoid, and influenza plagues, Great Britain listened to the admonitions of reformer Edwin Chadwick, who correlated poor living conditions and disease. Similarly, Massachusetts created its own Sanitary

Commission in 1850 and subsequently, in the same year that Riverside was planned, the Massachusetts State Board of Health. Other states formed their own boards, with the American Public Health Association created in 1872. Germ theory was in its infancy during this time, with the popular "miasma theory" (which attributed illness to bad night air) prevailing. Most popular writings of the time concurred that nature and the outdoors could improve public health.

Olmsted worked with many leading physicians and sanitary experts of the day, both in his park designs and to satisfy his insatiable curiosity about technical advances for health. George Waring Jr., a leading sanitation engineer, collaborated with Olmsted in designing the drainage of Central Park. These efforts, and Olmsted's managerial skill in Central Park, prompted clergyman Henry Whitney Bellows to suggest Olmsted as leader of the nation's Sanitary Commission (the predecessor to the Red Cross) during the Civil War.[28] Olmsted's belief that nature imparted health to humankind was reflected in his observation that "parks are now as much a part of the *sanitary* apparatus of a large town as aqueducts and sewers."[29]

TRENDS IN COMMUNITY PLANNING

Olmsted's childhood sensibilities and diverse careers contributed to his success as a landscape architect. His farming taught him horticultural techniques, journalism exposed him to landscapes and agriculture across the country, and publishing helped him establish contacts in the literary and philosophical world. And as important as this background, the era in which Olmsted came of age shaped his vision of suburban ideals. Major worldwide events such as industrialization and the overcrowding of cities helped fuel new ideas in how communities should be designed.

Attitudes toward rural and urban life shifted during the early and mid-1800s. As the United States changed from an agrarian to an industrial economy, so changed the population centers. The Industrial Age brought factory workers to the city, and waves of European immigrants furthered the overcrowding. Early advocates of the agrarian life, such as Thomas Jefferson, had emphasized its inherent self-reliance so necessary to a republic. Later, as author David Schuyler notes, this traditional thinking evolved into a nostalgic view of farming for its natural scenery.[30] Landscape artist Thomas Cole created a series of paintings, *The Course of Empire*, which depicted the beauty of pastoral, rural life and ended with the horrors of destruction in cities. Writers such as Henry David Thoreau and Ralph Waldo Emerson, both transcendentalist philosophers from New England and Olmsted confreres, believed strongly in the powers of Nature writ large. Yet, there was culture, art, and intellectualism in the cities. How could the ideals of the wholesomeness of the country be combined with the culture and proximity of the city?

The Cemetery Movement

Among the first attempts to blend nature with urban environment were the creations of rural cemeteries and, later, parks. Following a European trend, rural or country cemeteries began to replace urban graveyards in the 1830s. Health and economic reasons drove the change. City land was much more expensive than rural plots, and physicians began implicating urban cemeteries in public health crises such as yellow fever.[31] Public leaders began creating cemeteries outside of the city limits, buoyed by accessibility through the nascent railroads. Mount Auburn Cemetery, in Boston, was the nation's first rural cemetery founded in 1831. At the urging of physician Jacob Bigelow, and managed by the new Massachusetts Horticultural Society, the cemetery offered families a healthful, beautifully landscaped setting for contemplation. Grounds were laid out with curving roads and generously appointed plantings of trees and shrubs. As Schuyler notes, a major tenet of Romanticism, an idealistic view of nature, stated that such an environment soothed the soul and mind.[32] In keeping with this ideal, landscapes were designed to emulate nature.

Other cities followed the rural cemetery trend. In 1838, leaders in Brooklyn, New York, developed Greenwood Cemetery. Laurel Hill Cemetery in Philadelphia, created in 1836, overlooks the Schuylkill River and blooms with abundant greenery. Spring Grove Cemetery, organized by the Cincinnati Horticultural Society in 1844, also offers a tranquil landscape. Although Chicago had just recently been incorporated as a city in 1837, founders of its Rosehill Cemetery (1859) and Graceland Cemetery (1860) quickly adopted the cemetery movement for reasons of public health and landscape beauty. By the late 1840s, A. J. Downing hailed rural cemeteries as a remarkable example of public taste and noted that "the true secret of the attraction lies in the natural beauty of the sites . . . the united charm of nature and art—the double wealth of rural and moral associations."[33]

The Naturalistic Park Era

Downing drew the link between cemeteries and public parks. He and Olmsted, like many others, saw the benefits of public parks in England and other European countries. Those parks, typically former estates of wealthy landholders, hailed a progressive move toward the mingling of different economic groups. Downing, and later Olmsted, saw this as a great social reform and also as an opportunity to improve the morality and civility of the average working man.

American cities certainly enjoyed green spaces before this. Savannah, Georgia, designed in 1733 by English nobleman James Oglethorpe, featured green squares interspersed among the grid layout. A visitor to the town in 1808 observed, "The streets are wide and open into spacious squares, each of which has a pump in the centre, surrounded by a small plantation of trees." William Penn famously envisioned his plan for Philadelphia as a "green country town."[34] Penn, reacting both to prevailing urban unsanitary conditions and to the Great Fire of London in 1666, thought open space would be both healthful and fire-resistant. Open green spaces were to call to mind the "Moorefields," a marshy area outside London's wall and the countryside.[35] Much earlier, the street design of St. Augustine, Florida, emanated from a large, centrally located plaza, as did many early New England towns around a public town square.

Thus, while there may have been earlier American precedents for urban public parks, the intentional naturalistic park design began with Central Park in New York City. Downing is credited with the first public exhortation for a people's park in New York, but there had been decades of thinking about nature and green space before the competition for the park began in 1858. Unlike previous gardenesque parks, which Olmsted decried as an odd mixture of nature and art, Central Park would separate man-made structures from landscape effects.

Park mania swept across the United States, and Olmsted himself may have coined the term the American "park movement."[36] He and Vaux, along with their contemporaries, were in demand for park design. With the triumph of Central Park, the Olmsted firm planned thirty major park systems in the United States.[37] In short order, the Olmsted and Vaux names became the most sought-after in public and private community and landscape design. In 1869, the same year dated on the Riverside General Plan, Illinois adopted legislation authorizing three park districts in Chicago. The South Park District would be designed by Olmsted and the West by William Le Baron Jenney (who supervised the Riverside implementation). The ideals of park design were definitely on the mind of Riverside's investors.

SUBURBIA: BEST OF CITY AND RURAL ATTRIBUTES

Rural cemeteries brought city dwellers out to civilized versions of nature, and public parks brought nature to the city. But neither offered a solution for domesticity, the nineteenth-century catchphrase for a moral, peaceable home. As cities grew larger and more noisome and as transportation options increased, the search for a perfect suburb ensued.

Suburbs were not a new idea. In the 1800s, American theorists spawned a number of utopian villages, following principles of transcendentalism or religious communities. Most were short-lived, such as Brookfarm (1841), Hopedale (1842), and Fruitlands (1843), Massachusetts; or, in the Midwest, New Harmony, Indiana (1814), or Bishop Hill, Illinois (1846). While these experimental communities often stressed agrarian lifestyles, many espoused doctrines such as communal property rights, feminism, or other ideas uncommon at the time. Aside from these experimental communities, many unplanned farm villages of the mid-1800s often grew organically around a river that powered a gristmill or sawmill.

U.S. suburban community plans often followed England's model of suburbs. Robert Fishman notes how the examples of Victoria Park, Manchester (1836), Calverley New Town (ca. 1827), and Prince's Park, Liverpool (1842) influenced the development of Llewellyn Park, New Jersey, often considered America's first suburb.[38] Llewellyn Park, designed by architect Alexander Jackson Davis in 1857 for businessman Llewellyn Haskill, began with 350 acres of woodland centered by a 50-acre public park, the "Ramble." Expansive lots of 5 to 10 acres were sold to wealthy families to share

in the upscale neighborhood. Credit for the actual design of the Ramble landscape is unclear, which included picturesque, gardenesque, and pastoral elements.[39]

The differences among these earlier iterations of suburbs and that of Riverside are both subtle and important. Victoria Park, for example, conceived by a partnership of architects, included bespoke homes surrounded by large grounds. As Fishman notes, however, the individual estates in the suburb were surrounded by tall walls. This did not contribute to a democratic community vision. Llewellyn Park, while centered by a single public park, retained the natural beauty of the land but lacked sidewalks along the roads like the ones in Riverside, which allowed homeowners flexibility in neighborliness.

Chicago, the fastest-growing city of the time, still had abundant vacant land outside its urban core and was prime for suburban development. The railroad system in Chicago grew exponentially, reflecting the importance of Chicago as a hub connecting rail and water shipping. Contemporary author Everett Chamberlin recounted, "Of railroad mileage actually in operation, Chicago is accorded as her tributaries more than one-seventh of all the tracks laid on the Continent."[40] While many of these lines were devoted to freight, commuter trains ran on Chicago's north, west, and south sides.

In his 1874 book, real estate booster Chamberlin described more than sixty "suburbs" of Chicago. Of these, many antebellum outlying Chicago towns had been founded by individual or small partnerships of landholders/developers (for example, Hyde Park, Lakeview) and shared characteristics of a suburb, including large lots and rural prospects. However, these separate villages merely extended the grid street system and numbering from the city and would ultimately be annexed into Chicago in 1889. Always ripe for real estate investments, the Chicago area beckoned speculators.

Chamberlin wrote of the ubiquity and "inevitability" of "Improvement Companies": "But the eye of the far-seeing speculator alighted upon the spot, and the inevitable Company having been organized, the car of progress was speedily set in motion."[41] These speculative improvement companies were profit-motivated, in contrast to the later civic organizations (such as garden clubs and chambers of commerce) that espoused beautification through landscaping.

Indeed, investor consortiums developed several competing suburbs at about the same time as Riverside: Ravenswood (1868), Highland Park (1867), Norwood Park (1869), and Rogers Park (1871).[42] Of those, only Highland Park (laid out by landscape gardener H. W. S. Cleveland and partner W. R. French) remained an independent suburb, the remainder annexed into Chicago. Unlike Riverside, the assimilated suburbs had been laid out with grids (although Norwood Park did have an ellipse) and lacked the commitment to greenswards. Highland Park, with Cleveland's help, included curvilinear streets and greenery but was formed by joining two prior settlements, Port Clinton and St. John. Lake Forest, designed in 1857, included landscaping effects but was intended as a summer resort. None of these Chicago railroad suburbs, however, featured the philosophical underpinnings that Olmsted used in developing Riverside.

EXEMPLAR OF BEST PRACTICES IN RIVERSIDE

Because Olmsted implemented the best practices of the day in Riverside and worked with an undeveloped canvas of land and because of its enduring design, the village is widely recognized as America's most influential pioneering suburb. After interviewing hundreds of scholars and historians, the editors at the national Public Broadcasting System listed Riverside among the "10 Towns That Changed America." In the documentary of the same name,

Riverside received acclaim because "it serves as a record of what 'ideal' looked like for the first suburban commuters."[43] David Schuyler writes, "Because of its comprehensive design and national influence the most important suburb developed in the immediate postbellum years was the community of Riverside, Illinois."[44] Historian Kenneth Jackson asserts that, while Olmsted and Vaux laid out sixteen suburbs in their careers, the "first and most influential residential creation was Riverside."[45] Jackson further notes that "Riverside was acclaimed as the most complete realization of Olmsted's conception of a proper residential district," and its picturesque surroundings ultimately attracted "'the more intelligent and more fortunate classes.'"[46]

These accolades are well-earned. The challenge is, and has been, how to preserve the brilliant design and execution of a model suburb into the expectations and living conditions of today.

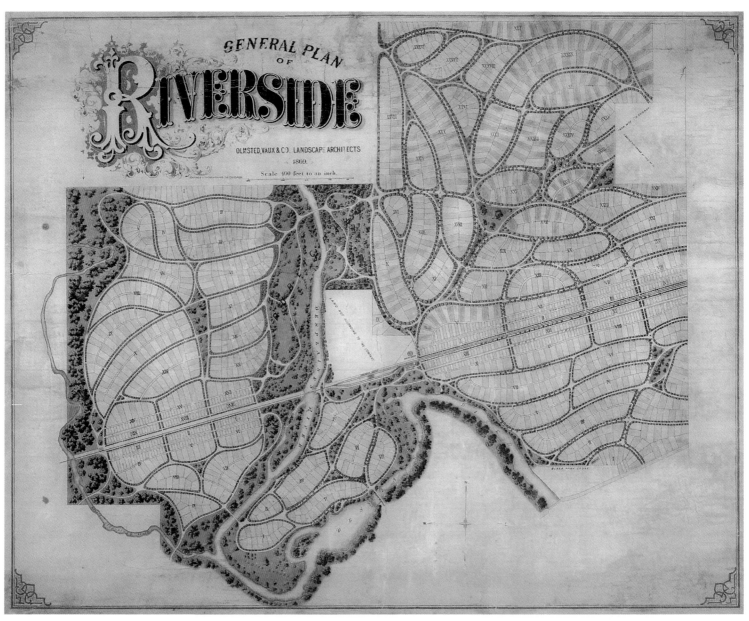

Olmsted and Vaux's General Plan of Riverside centered on the Des Plaines River. Except for a small portion west of the river, only the east side (right side on this map) was built. Village of Riverside, Riverside Historical Commission.

CHAPTER 2

The Genius of the Plan, Job #607

What makes Riverside a National Historic Landmark District, and why is it a worthy model for today's community designers? Riverside's design, identified in the Olmsted office files as Job #607, dramatically upended existing city planning.[1] The design of this master-planned community not only combined the benefits of city and rural living but also embodied the mid-nineteenth-century philosophical ideals of democracy, harmony with nature, and homeownership. Just as these ideals have endured, so has the Riverside design.

Suburbs like Riverside marked a new era in American community planning, geared less toward ideals of utopian communal living and founded more by investors than by philosophical iconoclasts. The National Park Service defines this period of historic suburbs as between 1830 and 1960.[2] It straddled the emergence of steam engine–powered travel through the World War II building boom. Early suburban communities of the mid-1800s relied on mass transportation to a nearby city. Thus, Riverside, strategically located on the Chicago, Burlington and Quincy Railroad (CB&Q) and snuggled within the embrace of the Des Plaines River, offered tremendous site advantages.

THE GENERAL PLAN: A BIT "BOSKY"

The Des Plaines River, sandwiched by a large "Public Park," as labeled on Olmsted and Vaux's General Plan of Riverside, divides the prospective site almost in half, east to west. Except for a small section west of the river, only the east portion of the land on the General Plan was purchased from David Gage, then owner of the farm tract. The west portion of the plan never became part of Riverside. While the interior of the plan is remarkable for its curving roads and green spaces, the external boundaries on the east and north are sharp-edged. This is likely because the original tract—including undeveloped land—overlays almost the entire portion of a square-mile township section, which was laid out in squares by military surveyors. Even today, the separate legal entity of Riverside Township almost perfectly overlays the Village of Riverside.

Although Olmsted refers in writing to the 1,600 acres to be developed (that lying mostly to the east of the river), as shown on the General Plan, clearly the Riverside Improvement Company (RIC) aspired to develop the western half.[3] (The RIC consisted of a group of men who invested in Riverside as a speculative profit-making endeavor.) When the western half of the proposed village could not be acquired, the Des Plaines River itself became the western and southern boundary of today's Riverside, as opposed to its central feature.[4] Olmsted envisioned the river as a major source of recreation and planned walkways along the banks for residents to enjoy its naturalistic beauty.

While there are some precedents to Riverside in the United States (Llewellyn, New Jersey, for example), none provides the breadth of innovative ideas. Originally farmland and later

Riverside's trees, mostly native, shelter humans and wildlife alike in the village's green spaces. Photo by author.

encompassing a thoroughbred horse track, the Riverside site offered a blank canvas for Olmsted's design for an ideal suburban community. Unlike Llewellyn or even Chicago suburb Lake Forest, the layout of the land was not guided by hills and ravines. Compared with those communities, Riverside is essentially flat, with a few ridges remaining from a long-ago beach head. Olmsted drew on this canvas his vision of an ideal suburb, and these signature elements described below have contributed to the village's success over the past 150 years.

Trees and Green Space

In a letter to his wife, Mary, Olmsted brainstormed names for the new suburb, further revealing his design intent. Rejecting the name "Riverside Park," he explained, "The river should be the important circumstance as the centre of improvements. I am willing to make it a river park but not a park. . . All of the Old English river names are out of my head. River Groves is the best that has occurred to me but a more bosky word than grove would perhaps be better."[5] Despite the many times Riverside has been idealized as a "village in a park," it is not so. Olmsted argued in his own *Preliminary Report upon the Proposed Suburban Village at Riverside* that a park must have range—that is, openness, seemingly unfettered by boundaries. Such range could not be achieved in an area dotted with private homes. In his report he said, "The greater part of your Riverside property has hardly any specially good conditions for a park, while it has many for a suburb."[6] Nor is Riverside a "village in a forest," a tagline sometimes used today. Although trees figured prominently in the design, and he preferred a "bosky" reference, a forest, in the 1860s, still resonated with wild imagery, possible danger, and uncouth civilization: definitely not an impression that Chicago investors wanted.

The slow-moving, curving river brought visual interest and abundant nature to the chosen site for Riverside. The river, however, not completely benign, caused Riverside residents to share causes with neighboring towns. Flooding from the Des Plaines River affected many in the Chicago area. In 1872, a major flood caused the Des Plaines to overload the Chicago River with its effluent. This undesirable overflow spotlighted a need for sanitary and drainage measures. In the Riverside area, the volume of water in the Des Plaines River was marked by significant highs and lows. One study reported, "The extreme low water volume on the Des Plaines, as measured at Riverside, in 1887 was 4 cubic feet per second; the flood volume of the same year, 10,324 cubic feet."[7]

Students of geology might wonder why the Des Plaines River makes such a sharp northeast turn at the southwest corner of Riverside. Riverside itself includes several sandy ridges, thought to

The Des Plaines River surrounds Riverside on two sides and became Olmsted's primary design element. Photo by William Suriano.

be remains of the Calumet beach during the glacial period of Lake Chicago. Large quarrying operations extracting hard stone have a long history in Lyons, near the southern edge of Riverside. But the hairpin turn of the river is not due to stone outcrops, according to an early geologist: "As no bed rock is exposed in the river bank, however, it is altogether probable that the recurving of the river to Riverside was brought about not by the resistance of rock encountered in the river bed, but rather by the initial slope of the old lake floor around the elevation."[8]

The bend of the Des Plaines River approaches extremely flat land between it and the south fork of the Chicago River. In times of spring floods, this area, known as Mud Lake, often proved an obstacle to pioneer travelers who hoped to connect from the Great Lakes to the Mississippi. The famous Chicago Portage, a land bridge connecting the Chicago and Des Plaines Rivers, used by early explorers including Marquette and Joliet, is within a stone's throw and helped put Riverside on the map. Early taverns and trading posts were built near the portage, and hence the area that would become Riverside became a familiar safe haven in times of rains that rendered the Chicago area unnavigable.

Witnessing firsthand the extent of floods, a *Chicago Tribune* reporter took the train to Riverside and Lyons after a springtime flood in April 1881. On the outbound CB&Q, crossing miles of flooded prairie—not due to river overflows but to the still-frozen,

Riverside's curving roads and walkways wend through a certified arboretum of trees, offering different views at every turn. Photo by author.

hard clay soil—the reporter noted "trees and fences rearing out of the water." Riverside, some fifteen feet higher than the surrounding area, seemed spared, with dust still lingering on its roads. Driving in a buggy with Riverside resident Dr. J. L. Congdon, the duo surveyed nearby towns. In Lyons, the Des Plaines had washed away homes and stores, skiffs were tied to telephone poles, and the "river proper was one broad expanse of water relieved here and there by the tops of bushes or a clump of trees."[9]

When not a rain-infused source of social change, the Des Plaines River functioned as Olmsted intended: to offer visual delight and restful entertainment.

Curvilinear Roads, to "Suggest and Imply Leisure"

Today, we take for granted the cul-de-sacs and curved roads of modern subdivisions. Riverside's design pioneered this effect in the flat plains of the Midwest and in most other early suburbs throughout America. Riverside is best experienced by driving or walking through its signature winding roads and sidewalks. The leisurely passage supports Olmsted's philosophy of the "unconscious," that the beauty of the surroundings would unfold gradually, in vignettes of nature revealed and concealed as observers traversed through the village. It is how Olmsted himself first learned to appreciate nature as a child—by taking long drives through country scenery with his father.

The genius of Olmsted's design—the placement of green spaces, the sunken serpentine roads, the glimpses of river—is in its flexibility despite the passage of years. Today, Riverside speed limits are twenty-five miles per hour—almost five times the rate a horse and carriage might have achieved, yet the evolving scenery continues to charm. As an experiment, car drivers can reduce car speed to about five miles per hour to better appreciate how the scenery might have looked while traveling by horse 150 years ago.

Even at a greater speed, which Olmsted may or may not have contemplated, the vistas are equally powerful.

Riverside became known for its winding roads—unusual in the flat Midwest. Road design, seemingly prosaic, could build or bust a new town. Landscape designers such as Andrew Jackson Downing heralded the curve as being in harmony with nature. Engineers of the day, however, preferred straight roads, particularly in the Midwest, where flat terrain promoted direct routes. Olmsted was quite clear on his preference for curved roads over straight, noting in his *Preliminary Report* on Riverside that "celerity will be of less importance than comfort and convenience of move." The goal of the road design was to "to suggest and imply leisure, contemplativeness and happy tranquility."[10] The arcs of Riverside's curving roads are exquisitely and mathematically formulated to create ample space at the interstices for small green spaces and to promote leisurely driving. Other suburban developers, such as those for the nearby "Cushing's Addition," who tried to emulate these curves "cut corners," resulting in anxiety-raising hairpin turns.

Aside from their sinuous curves, Riverside's roads, by design, exemplified state-of-the-art construction techniques, made to withstand freeze/thaw cycles and floods. The design anticipated drainage requirements with inobtrusive side cobblestone gutters (since Olmsted disliked the look of high curbs). Roads were depressed into the ground so that they disappeared from view when one looked across a common. The latest technology in macadam surfacing, using an imported steamroller, as prescribed by Olmsted, helped assure the roads would survive many winters and spring floods. Drainage also reduced the likelihood of standing water and attendant mosquitoes, which brought the dreaded ague. Solid construction design of the roads helped attain Olmsted's goal of a healthful suburb.

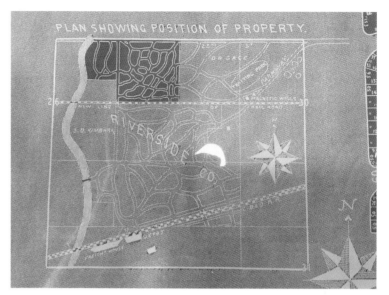

Cushing's Addition, a proposed but unrealized new suburb (now part of the separate village of North Riverside), copied the curving roads of Riverside. The Newberry Library, Plan of Cushman's Riverside Subdivision from *Landowner*.

Setbacks and Sidewalks for "Domestic Seclusion"

Olmsted insisted on generous setbacks for houses from the road, noting that "the front line of lots, and consequently that the roadside houses, must be placed at much greater distance from the wheelways than is usual or necessary in our city streets." This would give a more "rural" effect and "domestic seclusion."[11] This separation of the private from the public space helped Olmsted achieve the contrasting goals of domesticity and community. Community could be attained through strolls on the public sidewalks, but when one wanted to retreat into the peaceful home, it was suitably separated from the street. The trade-off—greater distance from the street to the front door—could be rectified with private roads (driveways) to the front door, per Olmsted. Setbacks were drawn in

Riverside roads were depressed below the landscape to cause them to "disappear" from sight. Here is the intersection of Longcommon and Nuttall in 1886. Village of Riverside, Riverside Historical Commission.

varying distances from the road, thus effecting an irregular pattern of open space as one travels the curving streets of Riverside.

Lot sizes were generous; the smallest boasted 100 feet of road frontage and 200 feet in depth. This further achieved a rural quality to the homesite, unlike the rowhouses previously popular in upper-class enclaves. Olmsted also proposed protecting the suburb from "ugly and inappropriate" architecture, writing, "We can require that no house shall be built within a certain number of feet of the highway, and we can insist that each home-holder shall maintain one or two living trees between his house and his highway-line."[12] Today, the requirement for two trees on the parkway still exists.[13]

Olmsted aimed to salvage existing trees as much as possible throughout the development. In this he followed the examples of Sir Uvedale Price and A. J. Downing. Upon first surveying the "as-is" condition of the land, Olmsted noted, "The more elevated parts of the ground, and the banks of the river everywhere, are occupied by groves of trees consisting of oaks, elms, hickories, walnuts, limes and ashes, with a scattered undergrowth of hazels, and various shrubs."[14] These groves were protected. His few notes

Modern-day view of Longcommon and Nuttall. Roads still remain "sunken" despite multiple resurfacings over the decades. Note the proliferation of distracting signage, often government-required. Photo by author.

on plantings for Riverside include some suggestions for tree group-ings, based largely upon the naturally predominating tree species. For example,

> In planting the long common and adjoining borders, oaks and elms should frequently stand alone or a little detached from groups, more frequently alone than anywhere else on the place except Indian Garden [a natural area near the river] where elms will [be] likely to grow particularly well. . . . In groups where oaks are intended to predominate[,] elms, especially the stiffer European sorts, may be introduced[.] Chestnuts also associate very agreeably with all oaks—better than with elms, so do the maples generally, and the maples better with chestnut than with elms. The American lime [linden tree, likely *Tilia americana*] very agreeably with either of the above. Dogwood and alder and I should think the common *crataegus* of Riverside would well with oak and all of the above.[15]

Olmsted's notes suggest an intentional artistic effect, along with horticultural appropriateness. Thus, in the same writing, when he recommends combining nettle trees and hornbeams with elms, it is because "they are good for tailing down a group of elms being of lower growth and somewhat like form with but little variety of color." Even Olmsted could not always articulate why he liked the effect of some groupings over others: "The horse chestnut associates more quietly with the limes than with any other tree I think. I hardly know why and it may be more associative with other pleasant circumstances in my mind."[16]

Olmsted's planting design principles, according to Olmsted scholar Charles Beveridge, aimed to create a sense of perspective, with the mix of foreground plantings and lighter-colored distance plantings creating illusions of space. The types of plants used were both practical and artistic. Per Beveridge, "[Olmsted] used many plants that were already part of the landscape character of the place and he knew they would thrive with little care. Still, he was anxious to enrich the natural scenery, and to do so he was willing to employ any thrifty plant that would add richness and variety without striking the average viewer as unnatural or exotic."[17]

Connection to the City

Although the newly established CB&Q Railroad offered passage from Riverside to the city, Olmsted counseled the Riverside Improvement Company to build a boulevard from Chicago to Riverside. This connecting road, he hoped, would be a major improvement to the environs and would further his goal of offering a democratic venue for all classes to enjoy. Referring to the "total lack of carriage drives leading from the city," the *Chicago Tribune* noted, "At one season of the year horses sink to their fetlocks, and broken [axles] are the penalties of attempting to drive out of the city. At another season, ruts, hobbles and hillocks absolutely preclude travel, and the consequence is that all pleasure driving is confined to a brief portion of Michigan avenue."[18]

Permission from Cook County authorities to construct this boulevard was written into the RIC bylaws, contingent on the land sales from private landowners along the route. But the land purchases stalled, and the boulevard was never built as Olmsted imagined it: a promenade for carriages, bridle paths, and pedestrians where all members of society could democratically mingle. This promenade Olmsted saw as crucial to his ideal of Riverside—it would help build a sense of community and would also encourage commuters and residents to travel to and from the village. Anticipating future growth of cities, the boulevard would also link to other parks in Chicago, similar to Boston's Emerald Necklace.

The lack of the main promenade caused and even today causes some curious unintended consequences. Today there is no obvious "front door" to Riverside, although Olmsted likely intended the gateway to be the junction of the unrealized boulevard with Longcommon Road. Over the years, various entrances have been created; today there are about twenty, most opening east to Harlem Avenue. No entrance road is particularly significant, and thus, perhaps, Riverside has remained under the radar for decades.

The area surrounding Riverside at inception consisted of flat farmland or uncultivated prairie. Although there are some ill-defined street terminuses onto what is today Harlem Avenue, the majority of ingress/egress points on the General Plan are sited near the river. On the plan, there are six bridges across the river into Riverside, yet only three exist today: at Ogden Avenue, Joliet Avenue, and the Burlington Northern Railroad trestle. All of these preexisted Riverside. The General Plan included a bridge across Salt Creek into the public park, another across that park into the First Division, and yet another across the public park onto Delaplaine Road.

If we discount the preexisting entryways, it would seem that Olmsted wanted visitors to enter the main circulation roads of Riverside (Delaplaine and Scottswood to Longcommon) through a beautiful park. And why not? According to a contemporaneous report, the most attractive area near Riverside—and thus an extension of Olmsted's ideal—lay along the river. Describing the riverbank area north of the village in early days, one resident recalled, "From the [railroad] bridge to the cemeteries was a forest. A dense woods stood from Harlem Road to the river, and between Forest avenue and the Suburban tracks which was known as the Beebe Sub-division and which contained hundreds of black walnut and butternut trees. Luscious berry bushes abounded and game was still to be found."[19]

By virtually any city planning wish list of the era or later, Olmsted and Vaux's General Plan included elements of a desirable master-planned community. Consider the Garden City and City Beautiful movements (beginning around the 1890s): these city planning theories promoted a democratic good philosophy, also consistent with Olmsted's Riverside goals, and a holistic combination of green space with roads and architecture. New Urbanism goals are also well-represented in Riverside: walkability, sustainability, transit corridors, cultural opportunities, land conservation, distributed range of parks, and so on.[20] Landscape urbanism proposes pockets of greenery interwoven with the built environment. Today's challenges of climate change emphasize a town's resiliency, water needs or excess, and carbon sequestration. While Riverside is not subject to the extremes of the coasts, its location, chosen by Olmsted, infrastructure in drainage and flood control, and abundance of green space make it as highly adaptable to climate change as any other suburb.

SEVEN S'S OF OLMSTED'S DESIGNS

Foremost Olmsted scholar Charles Beveridge identified the seven critical elements of all of Olmsted's designs, each beginning with

Nature's Beauty Spot.   Riverside, Ills.

This postcard from around 1900 shows the naturalistic view of the river. As the postcard writer notes, the river was still clean for swimming and fishing. Author's collection.

the letter S.[21] Below is a description of how all of these elements are embedded in Riverside's design.

Scenery

Beveridge describes "passages of scenery" that constantly open up to new views and avoid "hard-edge or specimen planting." Whether driving or walking in Riverside, the curves in the roads and sidewalks partially obscure what is around the bend and create a sense of anticipation. Olmsted and other designers refer to this as a sense of mystery. As seasons change, as plants grow and change color, it is true that the alternate open views with counterpoint enclosures delight the senses. Riversiders have overwhelmingly voiced appreciation for the changing vistas in survey after survey.

The success of Riverside's design was immediately apparent. In addition to "copycat" suburbs such as Cushing's Addition, many developers, yesterday and today, have adopted the curvilinear street structure. The notion of hiring a landscape architect to help plan a new development or even a private residence took on a certain cachet.

Suitability

Suitability refers to designs that respect the natural topography, per Beveridge, and evoke the "genius of the place." Olmsted selected the Riverside site for its natural features and made the river and groves of trees along the commons central to his design. The naturalistic design emphasized the natural wooded areas of the commons and the serpentine path of the river.

Style

Beveridge notes that Olmsted designed in "specific styles, each for a particular effect," with the "Pastoral" style (open greensward with small bodies of water and scattered trees and groves) for a soothing, restorative atmosphere, or the "Picturesque" style (profuse planting, especially with shrubs, creepers, and ground cover on steep and broken terrain) "for a sense of the richness and bounteousness of nature, with chiaroscuro effects of light and shade." Scholar and author Malcolm Cairns notes that the Pastoral style of landscape design, "rounded, smooth, relaxing and therapeutic," predominated in Riverside.[22]

Isolating and pigeonholing a style can be difficult: there are other styles of which Olmsted was aware, including the so-called Beautiful and Formal. In Riverside, the areas bordering the Des Plaines River generally exhibit a naturalistic, nearly Picturesque design, with trees unmanicured and areas such as Picnic Island allowed to grow naturally. Areas surrounding residences, such as the smaller parks, are planted primarily with turf and trees, reflecting the "Pastoral" style.

Olmsted, in his *Preliminary Report*, described the river's Picturesque scene: "The banks of the river everywhere, are occupied by groves of trees consisting of oaks, elms, hickories, walnuts, limes and ashes, with a scattered undergrowth of hazels, and various shrubs; most of the trees are young, but there are many specimens of large size and umbrageous form."[23]

Olmsted envisioned the river walk area as a great source of pleasure: "A public drive and walk should be carried near the edge of the bank in such a way as to avoid destroying the more valuable trees growing upon it, and there should be pretty boat-landings, terraces, balconies overhanging the water, and pavilions at points desirable for observing regattas, mainly of rustic character, and to be half overgrown with vines."[24]

Throughout the decades, as will be described in subsequent chapters, the walks along the river have varied in their accessibility, desirability, and compatibility with Olmsted's intent. As of today, there are some areas that are consistently troubled by invasive plants, river flooding, and poor trails. A very recent effort is underway to commingle active and passive recreation by installing a disc golf course in the middle of the public greenway. Yet, other areas have been greatly improved through stewardship and natural areas management.

Subordination

Defined by Beveridge as "subordination of all elements, all features and objects, to the overall design," this is the quintessential ingredient to the Riverside design. Excepting the so-called central business district (which was a later addition to Olmsted's design), all of the public land is subject to ordinances and a Landscape Advisory Commission. Brightly colored, man-made objects that would detract from the natural scene are discouraged.

Separation

The separation of areas was created by different design styles, so that an "incongruous mixture of styles" would not dilute the intended effect of each: for example, a separation of ways, in order to ensure safety of use and reduce distractions for those using the space; or a separation of conflicting or incompatible uses. Sidewalks offer pathways for pedestrians; roads were created for carriages and, later, cars; river footpaths border swaths of greenspace; and the central business district, even as amended today, is isolated from the pastoral green space.[25]

Sanitation

"Provision for adequate drainage and other engineering considerations . . . promote both the physical and mental health of users." In 1869, particularly in the flat, clay soil around Chicago, drainage posed a major issue. Undrained, swampy areas threatened health with the potential for malaria. Poorly drained roads discouraged foot or wheel traffic. Olmsted, with his background with the U.S. Sanitary Commission and his knowledge of the park and rural cemetery movements, had a heightened awareness of health requirements when designing the community. His specifications for road building in Riverside and provision for cobblestone gutters to drain away standing water featured prominently in the *Preliminary Report*.

Service

Beveridge noted Olmsted's designs served a "purpose of direct utility or service." Ornamental elements were included only if they performed a useful function. Olmsted did not add any statuary or memorials in his design for Riverside, although he had to accommodate them in other works such as Central Park. The temptation for memorial structures or statuary is ever-present in Riverside; understandably, people want to commemorate events or individuals. However, the concern with memorials (such as statues of famous or locally prominent individuals, or colorful wayfaring signage) is that artificial, man-made objects would detract from the pure beauty of nature. Appointed commissions are now established in Riverside to protect the landscape and historic areas, but constant challenges to preservation persist.

Job #607 in the Olmsted files may exist only as an archival collection of correspondence and the seminal General Plan of Riverside. But, its living, breathing counterpart just ten miles west of Chicago reflects the enduring genius of Olmsted's design. The artist's brushstrokes rendered the masterwork; would its beneficiaries steward the fledgling treasure?

The river, railroad (depot seen in background), and provision of "artificial improvements" such as water and power lured prospective buyers to Riverside. Photo by William Suriano.

CHAPTER 3

Off the Drawing Boards (1869–1879)

The best design may never see the light of day if the implementation team is poorly chosen. Even with a seemingly well-qualified team, there may be instances where personal interests trump common goals. If the designer is still available, as Olmsted was at Riverside's inception, he or she can intercede for the greater good. Once the handoff from creator to investor is made, however, stewardship of the design begins—for better or worse. As Olmsted noted, "The architect and the gardener do not understand each other, and commonly the owner or resident is totally at variance in his tastes and intentions from both."[1] A meeting of the minds must ensue among planners, architects, owners, and landscape architects, or degradation of the design is likely to follow.

The birth of Riverside, in another era or place, might have been fumbled in the hands of lesser midwives or as a result of bad timing. Instead, all stars were aligned, from Chicago's real estate market, to financial conditions, to location, to the chance meeting of Frederick Law Olmsted and Emery E. Childs. Chicago in the late 1860s gleamed with opportunity. During the Civil War, the city, despite its sacrifice of many lives and livelihoods to the Union cause, nonetheless profited through its extensive railroad and grain exchange system supplying the troops. The Union stockyards opened in 1865, cementing the fortunes of meatpackers and ancillary businesses. Chicago's population nearly tripled between 1860 and 1870; the 1870 census counted almost 300,000 residents, straining the city's housing capacity and concentrating all the smoke, congestion, and offal in the newly industrialized metropolis. Suburbs, particularly those along the gleaming new railroad lines, offered an antidote to crowded urban streets.

The park movement also helped popularize the idea of nature as an antidote to urban turbulence. After the war, among his many endeavors, Frederick Law Olmsted encouraged like-minded advocates of health and culture to promote the parks system in Chicago. Fellow U.S. Sanitary Commission member and civic leader Ezra McCagg and physician John Rauch of Chicago's Board of Health joined others in passing state legislation creating the west, south, and north park divisions in Chicago. The park movement, active across the nation, linked health and nature with real estate opportunity.

Chicago's real estate market boomed. The embryonic beginnings of Riverside appeared in a small notice in the July 30, 1864, issue of the *Prairie Farmer*, a Chicago-based newspaper with wide circulation across the Midwest:

> Sale of a Farm: The Farm at Lyons, Cook county, formerly owned by B. F. Carver Esq., of this city, and known as the Carver farm, has been purchased by David A. Gage Esq. of the Sherman House, for the sum of 50,000 dollars. This farm is finely located on the Des Plaines river, has beautiful groves, and will be made one of the finest of western suburban residences. There is no more eligible location in this vicinity.[2]

Four years later, Gage personally estimated the property at ten times its 1864 sales price, not an outlandish claim given Chicago's red-hot real estate prices. In the first twenty years since the city's incorporation in 1837, land outside the city limits appreciated nearly tenfold.[3] Adding to Chicago's local property values, the new city park system, created through legislation in 1869, brought the benefits of green space to the city and pushed many speculative developments outside its boundaries.

Chicago's recent city improvements, such as widening its signature State Street, were dubbed a "Hausmannizing [sic]" effect, similar to the sanitation and beautification efforts by Georges-Eugène Haussmann, in Paris.[4] Proposed parks, city improvements, and the success of sanitary, landscaped cemeteries championed by Rauch, such as Rosehill (1859) and Graceland (1860) on Chicago's North Side, helped pave the way for local enthusiasm for nature-based suburbs. The remaining ingredients in this alchemy to produce Riverside were capital, a strategic location, visionary founders, homebuyers, an experienced implementation team, and, of course, the genius of Olmsted and his plan.

RIVERSIDE IMPROVEMENT COMPANY: "I WAS OVERCOME BY THE HONOR"

Olmsted estimated the cost of development of the 1,600 acres, assuming his involvement, would exceed $1 million (about $20 million today).[5] To raise this substantial sum, consistent with national trends, an investors' consortium, or "improvement company," was formed. As noted by architect Robert A. M. Stern, "Of the hundreds of village improvement societies founded in the second half of the nineteenth century, many were interested in the romantic goal of making their town more village-like."[6] With the plains around Chicago ripe for development, the Riverside Improvement Company enjoyed carte blanche in designing the new village.

Most writings about the RIC founders variously describe a group of Eastern businessmen. Actually, while the six founders were all born in New England, only two (Emery Childs and Leverett Murray) still lived there. The remaining four members hailed from Chicago (David Gage, William Allen, Henry Seelye, and George Kimbark). This is a crucial point because had Riverside been founded entirely by absentee landlords, its long-term survival might have been at greater risk. All RIC members were in their late thirties or forties with diversified investments and many careers behind them.[7] What brought this particular group of individuals together, and what unique blend of personalities wrought the initial success and subsequent quick demise of the RIC? What particular set of experiences or aesthetic predisposition induced the men to hire Olmsted for the design?

Childs and Gage

The initial sale of the Riverside property occurred between easterner Emery Childs and Chicagoan David Gage. Having Chicago political and social connections and listed as one of the richest men in Chicago, Gage was well-positioned to approach the other RIC Chicago-based founders—Allen, Seelye, and Kimbark—all of whom enjoyed substantial wealth.[8] Their names on the RIC letterhead added legitimacy to the operation.[9]

The critical sale of 1,100 acres of Gage's Riverside Farm to Childs for $300,000 occurred in July 1868. With less than 14 percent paid in up-front cash, the balance due Gage was speculative, based on lots sold. Gage would also receive an additional 10 percent of profits from the company.[10] Childs also paid $40,000 to landowner Eli Prescott for an additional 500 acres west of the Des Plaines, thus bringing Riverside's total acreage to 1,600, at an average price per acre of about $212, neither a bargain nor an excessive price, based on comparably undeveloped acres.[11] According

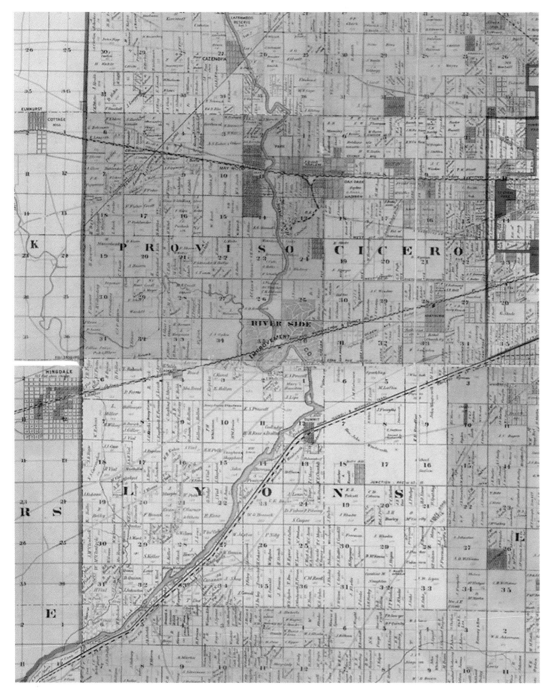

This county map of Riverside, ca. 1870, shows the western half platted, although it was not built. Surrounding areas remained largely farmland. Library of Congress. J. Van Vechten, *Van Vechten's Map of Cook and Du Page Counties Also the Northern Portion of Lake County, Indiana* (Chicago: J. Van Vechten, 1870), https://www.loc.gov/item/2013593087/.

to David Gage, the RIC issued shares to the other members of the RIC, to allow them directorships in the fledgling enterprise.[12]

Gage and Childs, the principal actors in this deal, met in 1868, when Gage discussed his plans to subdivide his property at Riverside Farm. According to Gage, Childs encouraged a grand vision for the subdivision, with macadamized roads and other improvements. Childs, in later court testimony, recalled the transaction differently, suggesting that he was pressured into the purchase through a combination of blandishments and salesmanship. "It came out . . . some way that [Riverside] was the only property about Chicago, that that was the only land there was. Well, somehow there was an excursion; we went down there one day to that farm

David A. Gage and Emery E. Childs met on an excursion to Riverside with other potential speculators and enjoyed a picnic near Swan Pond. This image, from around the 1890s or the next decade, shows the early water tower (background left), oxbow streamlet around Picnic Island, and hotel (background right). Chicago History Museum, ICHi.183246A.

and all the distinguished residents of Chicago that I had never seen before went down on that excursion and I was overcome by the honor that was given to me by that invitation, and I went." Childs continued his testimony about this first visit, casting himself as an innocent: "I was quite flattered, . . . I got quite excited about it, and as I got excited, Mr. Gage was entirely indifferent."[13]

Gage's apparent coyness belied the fact that he had frequently hosted excursions to the Riverside Farm with politicians and Chicago investors and had already drawn a map to subdivide the property. So, was Childs a naïf and Gage a huckster? Probably neither, or possibly both; certainly they shared flamboyant traits of the typical real estate investor in Chicago suburban properties in the late 1860s. The RIC itself would go bankrupt in a few years, its leadership accused of financial improprieties involving other companies (a gas works and a railroad) to hide ballooning debt.

Emery Childs, who would become president of the RIC, struck an unassuming figure with his sandy hair and hazel eyes and being of average height.[14] Like many investor-entrepreneurs, his résumé as of 1868 included a variety of jobs. In his early twenties, he toiled as a bookkeeper in his hometown of Hartford, Connecticut. (There is no evidence that Childs, about ten years younger than Olmsted, met the latter in Hartford. But the Olmsted name was well-known and might have influenced Childs's selection of the designer). In the mid-1850s, Childs became an absentee landlord and partner in a dry goods business (later dissolved with some enmity) in Keokuk, Iowa. By the 1860s, he had moved to Brooklyn, New York, where he established another dry goods partnership with six other men. During this time, he invested locally in real estate. At the time of the Riverside affair, Childs and his wife, Mary, had three young children.

David Gage dabbled in many pursuits. After the death of his first wife, the childless widower Gage relocated from

Massachusetts to Vermont, where he married his second wife, Eliza, in 1851. By 1860, he and his brother, George, moved to Chicago and quickly assimilated into the community, as part owners and managers of the popular Tremont House hotel and later the Sherman House. The brothers were not strangers to major construction and risk-taking: their Tremont House received acclaim for the engineering feat of being lifted in toto to match the street level in 1861. It took 500 men with 5,000 jackscrews, and lore says hotel business carried on as usual. The Tremont House and the Sherman House hosted the nation's leaders, and Gage could not help but rub elbows with Chicago's elite.

Extending his risk profile, Gage bred and raced trotting horses, with the Riverside Farm serving as a racetrack and auction site. Several of his stock were listed in *The American Stud Book*, the authority on thoroughbred horses. In another chancy enterprise, Gage entered a twenty-year partnership with Franklin Parmelee to operate Chicago's first horse-drawn rail line in 1854. Politically savvy, he secured a position on the Canal Commission and served as City of Chicago treasurer in 1863. In 1869, while incorporating the RIC, Gage also served as president of the Chicago White Stockings baseball team (ultimately, the Chicago Cubs) and won the election for a second term as Chicago's treasurer.

Perhaps the seminal meeting between Gage and Childs occurred during the holiday excursion Gage hosted on July 4, 1868. Gage invited about sixty prominent businessmen to his Riverside Farm for a day of relaxation and conviviality. After an hour's train ride, the group disembarked at Riverside to play cards at tables set up near the river, have lunch, and enjoy a barrel of punch. The men ambled to the horse track for an exhibition race and, after several speeches by local and state politicians, returned to Chicago by a seven o'clock evening train. This holiday celebration, the fourth of its kind, brought many a potential investor to Gage's farm.[15]

So, while Gage clearly wooed Childs and other investors, the connection with Olmsted is less obvious. Both Childs and Leverett Murray lived a stone's throw from Brooklyn's Prospect Park, Olmsted's latest design then under construction. The rise in nearby real estate values was tempting; one 1869 booklet estimated Brooklyn property values escalated nearly 30 percent over three years due to Prospect Park and prophesied that Chicago area properties could do the same.[16] Childs and Murray would have had firsthand experience with how improved parkland raised nearby real estate values.

Olmsted was renowned in Chicago, as well as in New York. His role as general secretary of the Sanitary Commission during the Civil War introduced him to many of Chicago's elite, such as lawyer and statesman Ezra McCagg, who orchestrated some of Chicago's most successful fundraisers, including the 1864 Northwestern Sanitary Fair, for the commission. A direct connection with David Gage is not known; however, Olmsted likely stayed at the Tremont or Sherman House during his Chicago sojourns.

With the Gage farmland sale completed in July, development plans raced forward. By August 20, barely a month after the sale, Olmsted traveled with John Bogart, Prospect Park's engineer, to Riverside to look over the land and begin contract negotiations with Childs. At this point, the RIC had not yet been formally incorporated, and Childs and Gage officially represented the venture. Olmsted, elbow-deep in several ongoing projects, arrived in Chicago after a whirlwind train trip from New York City, including a stopover in Buffalo to discuss park possibilities. Worn out, he recalled the trip in a letter to his wife, Mary: "I was ill when I reached Chicago but to keep my engagement drove 20 miles over open prairie, bleak & raw wind, & walked a good deal. Next day could not speak easily & had to keep my bed. Friday another 20 miles but this time in a close carriage. Got back late. Saturday, conferences, debates, rough plans, treaties about terms consumed the time till we had to run for the train."[17]

Olmsted prepared for the RIC the pivotal *Preliminary Report upon the Proposed Suburban Village at Riverside, Near Chicago* on September 1, 1868. This oft-quoted report laid out Olmsted and Vaux's principles of design and recommendations for Riverside. Just six weeks later, in mid-October, Olmsted delivered a plan

William Le Baron Jenney's architecture office co-listed with the Riverside Improvement Company office, registered at 73 Clark Street in Chicago (pre–Chicago Fire of 1871). Village of Riverside, Riverside Historical Commission. Address listing per *Edwards' Annual 14th Directory of the City of Chicago*, Internet Archive.

for 300 plots to Childs, who, according to Olmsted, impatiently awaited the drawings because "there was an eager demand for lots at Riverside at least $1000 a lot." This first drawing was of the so-called First Division, the southwest area that forms a peninsula wrapped by the river. Olmsted clearly had misgivings about the risk associated with the endeavor; writing in late August to his partner Calvert Vaux, he called Riverside "a big speculation."[18] By October 1869, he derided the whole project as "a regular flyaway speculation . . . [that] is managed on Gold Exchange and Erie principles."[19] Olmsted's concerns about his own compensation emerged as soon as November 1868, when he wrote his attorney with fears that Childs would not be able to pay the firm's bill.[20]

Olmsted's qualms about the RIC's solvency were well-founded as the company used several shell companies to transfer its liabilities. Childs created the Riverside Water and Gas Works and later the Chicago and Great Western Rail Companies to issue bonds and cover RIC debts. While neither Childs nor Gage was criminally charged in the Riverside enterprise, litigation followed them throughout their careers.[21] The Chicago Fire of 1871, followed by a national financial panic in 1873, nailed the coffin on the Riverside Improvement Company. It folded in 1873, with claims and counterclaims wending through the judicial system for years.

About twenty properties had been built in Riverside, most owned by wealthy Chicagoans with much to lose if the development failed. Streets had been improved with macadam only in the First and Second Divisions; the rest of the roads were just depressions in the ground. This could have been the end of Riverside just three years after its birth. Thankfully, enough men had invested in the property and believed in the vision such that they remained and incorporated the development as the Village of Riverside in 1875. The village now had a proper government organization. Would Olmsted's plan survive it?

THE IMPLEMENTATION TEAM: "CONSULT A TASTEFUL AND EXPERIENCED PROFESSIONAL"

As inspired as the General Plan was, the true test of a promising plan depends on those charged with installation. As Olmsted's direct involvement in the Riverside project diminished, the Riverside Improvement Company relied on the trusted firm of Jenney, Schermerhorn and Bogart to perform the actual construction of his plan. Assisted by hundreds of laborers, the firm translated Olmsted's plan into a physical landscape.[22]

William Le Baron Jenney, then thirty-seven, hailed from Massachusetts and had studied at Harvard and the École Centrale Paris. During the Civil War, he worked as an engineer for Generals W. T. Sherman and U. S. Grant. He and Olmsted first met in 1863 at Sherman's headquarters in Vicksburg during the war and enjoyed discussions on topics ranging from the art at the Louvre to slavery in the South.[23] Jenney moved to Chicago in 1867. Louis Y. Schermerhorn studied civil engineering in Troy, New York, at the Rensselaer Polytechnic Institute. He collaborated with Olmsted and Vaux on Prospect Park between 1866 and 1869.[24] John Bogart, who studied at Rutgers College, also worked at Prospect Park and became chief engineer there in 1870.[25] All three men therefore shared Olmsted's design goals and had previous experience with him.

The team leveraged new technologies such as a modern steamroller and patented tree pruner to expedite construction and create the naturalistic design that Olmsted sought. Construction crews raided many nearby groves for mature trees—those with diameters greater than four inches. In the winter of 1870, one visitor marveled at the work of a "gang of twenty-five men" who, with the aid of a custom truck "built expressly for this purpose on scientific principle," started digging into the "prairie portion of the property."[26] The unearthed trees, with their frozen balls of dirt, weighed

The Riverside Improvement Company built the Riverside Hotel, shown here ca. 1890s, to attract visitors and investors. Village of Riverside, Riverside Historical Commission.

as much as five to twenty tons and were transported, upright, from nearby forests to their location on the grounds. An estimated 2,000 trees from local forests, some twenty inches in diameter and 100 feet high, were planted in this manner.[27] The survival rate of such transplants must have been low, since today few professional foresters plant trees greater than a few inches in diameter.

In May 1870, Chicago nurseryman Edgar Sanders, known locally as the "Dean of Horticulturists," visited Riverside to see the operation himself. He consulted on-site with George Skinner, a forty-year-old New York native, responsible for tree transplanting. Skinner promoted himself as a "practical landscape gardener" with twenty-eight years of experience in English and American parks, notably working with Olmsted and Vaux as general foreman for Prospect Park.[28] Sanders noted, "We gleaned from Mr. G. Skinner,

Successful implementation of the General Plan required a superintendent such as William Le Baron Jenney, who sympathized with Olmsted's design aesthetic, including curving roads and naturalistic scenery. Photo by author.

the efficient manager, a few particulars of this gigantic tree planting operation. The whole extent of purchases so far, in the tree and shrub line, is some 20,000. . . . Of these 700 may be called giants of the forest, consisting of Oak, Linden, Elm, Maple, Ash, Cherry, Walnut Hickory, & c."[29]

Skinner had recently invented an extending ladder, used in Riverside to prune high branches of large trees, thus enhancing their viability. This capability would draw worldwide acclaim when demonstrated six years later at the 1876 Centennial Exposition in Philadelphia.[30] Called a "gentleman of considerable mechanical skill and knowledge" by the *Chicago Tribune*, Skinner, then living in Riverside, exhibited his ladder in Chicago for its potential in firefighting in January 1870.[31]

Local nurseries and horticulturists assisted in obtaining nursery stock and in the actual planting, which meant it is likely that nonnative plants were included in the installation. The DuPage Nursery, one of a handful of local nurseries, contracted with the RIC to supply nonnative evergreens. Based on its catalog of 1871, likely specimens included arborvitae, hemlock, pine, balsam fir, and Norway spruce. Sanders described some of the trees as being thirty feet tall with root balls nine feet in diameter, noting, "Each tree had to have a railroad truck of its own; and as we saw them late in the winter, under the process of being transported, the effect at a distance was like a moving forest."[32] Imagine the farmers along the CB&Q watching this parade of trees pass by their fields.

Skeptics critiqued Riverside's rejection of traditional street grids. The village's signature curved roads drew fire from Samuel S. Greeley, a Chicago engineer (who later partnered with Olmsted protégé H. W. S. Cleveland), when, before a conference of engineers, he singled out the village's layout as being impractical and inefficient. Schermerhorn took Greeley to task by noting that only a carelessly planned village might suffer that fate. To demonstrate his point, Schermerhorn measured the distance from each home in Riverside to the train depot, under both a curving road system and a hypothetical rectilinear plan, and he concluded that the curved roads proved more efficient by nearly 17 percent.[33]

Olmsted clearly wanted an architect with sympathetic taste in developing Riverside. William Le Baron Jenney fit the bill. Writing about the ideal suburban home in the *Riverside Gazette* in 1871, Jenney advised, "The architect of a suburban dwelling should be a landscape architect as well and design the house, grounds and outbuildings at the same time." As far as the house itself, Jenney urged restraint, suggesting that "simplicity is elegance." And, as pertained to the grounds themselves, he wrote, "Consult a tasteful and experienced professional; obtain a comprehensive plan, and have the work carried to completion under his direction. Above all let him take charge of the planting. It is seemingly the most easy, while it really requires the most knowledge. He must know the growth of the tree or plant, the character of the foliage, and in the case of border plants, the color of the flowers."[34]

Very few homeowners took Jenney's landscape advice, if the woodcuts of homes and gardens in an 1871 RIC promotional brochure are accurate. Most of the home grounds feature islands of fashionably colorful flowers. This attention-grabbing garden style expressly contradicted the naturalistic look Olmsted espoused. Of course, artistic license was likely involved on the part of the engraver, yet the RIC would have had to endorse the noncompliant etchings in the booklet.

For the most part, the RIC interpreted Olmsted's designs as recommended in *public* areas. RIC members embellished some guidelines and added their own touches. To reduce lot speculation and assure quality homes, they required lot purchasers to build within a year a home worth at least $3,000. They insisted that the front yard, between the thirty-foot setback and the road, be kept as

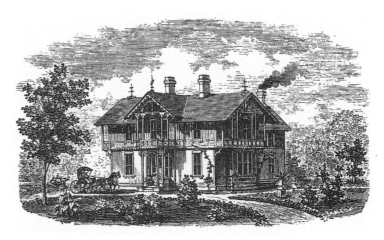

The RIC prospectus described the John C. Dore house, extant today, as a "low Swiss cottage." One of the oldest surviving Riverside structures, it was designed by Olmsted, Vaux & Co. Village of Riverside, Riverside Historical Commission.

an "open court or door yard," perhaps reinforcing the front-yard-as-lawn convention.[35] And, curiously, for picturesque effect, the RIC imported 100 English sparrows and handcrafted rustic birdhouses. The hope was that the birds would multiply rapidly, following a similar program in Richmond, Virginia, where 36 birds ultimately resulted in more than 500.[36] (This sparrow importation ultimately backfired. In 1912, a local editorial excoriated the overpopulation of English sparrows: "They are dirty, quarrelsome, voracious feeders and destructive. In short, they are pests.")[37]

The *Riverside Gazette*, written largely, it would seem, by Jenney and colleagues, offered tips for private landscapes. A newspaper illustration of the Leverett Murray grounds hints at how Olmsted might have designed a Riverside private garden. This large corner property on Nuttall Road, across from the Longcommon—the village's signature public green space—features massed groupings of shrubbery on the borders, a kitchen garden and outbuildings in

William Le Baron Jenney designed the "rural villa in Gothic style" for RIC secretary Leverett W. Murray. Village of Riverside, Riverside Historical Commission.

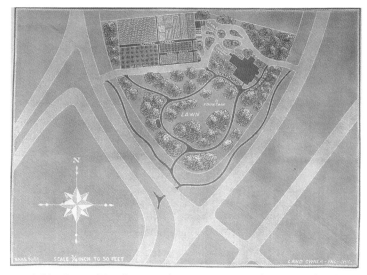

This 1870 etching from Landowner *magazine shows a garden design for the Murray house "from the pen of Frederick Law Olmsted." If offers insight as to how Olmsted might have designed Riverside private gardens.* Chicago History Museum, ICHi.183278.

back, and a plane of turf offsetting the plantings. Walkways meander through the property, consistent with Olmsted's point of view that a garden must be experienced through walking.

Although no fences are shown on this diagram, the outer belt of shrubbery preserved privacy, especially important for a home with two-sided exposure to the street. Olmsted did disapprove of "high dead-walls, as of a series of private mad houses, as is done in some English suburbs."[38] Writing to friend Edward Everett Hale in 1869, he noted, "You will see by the Berkeley & Riverside reports that I favor fences. . . . They are of great value as making emphatic the division of freehold property—the independence of the freeholder relatively to the public & to his neighbors. . . . I think that the want of fences, of distinct family separation out of the house, is the real cause of the ill-success or want of great success of [New York businessman] Mr. [Llewellyn Solomon] Haskell's undertaking at Orange, Llewellyn Park."[39] Today, Riverside has ordinances against front-yard fences.

Despite his reservations of the RIC management, Olmsted seemed pleased with the work of his team. On May 8, 1869, Olmsted himself led a tour of Riverside for about 500 prominent citizens of Chicago. A special train outfitted with Pullman cars, including dining rooms and comfortable coaches, left Chicago at 1 p.m. laden with Chicago aldermen, public works officials, and other leaders. About fifty carriages awaited the blue-ribbon group, including wives and daughters. Olmsted escorted the visitors through the grounds, noting, according to the *Chicago Tribune*, that "the land was both fertile and high, the Des Plaines River was unsurpassed for its general beauty, the forest was abundant and there was no good reason why Riverside Park should not be made the most attractive place on the continent."[40]

The village was open for business. Despite Olmsted's fears, sales prospects in 1869 seemed bright.

THE EARLY THREATS: "I AM SHOCKED AND PAINED"

The first risk to Olmsted's plan came quickly, within the first year of construction. The enemy came from within. Emery Childs either selfishly or unknowingly chose to desecrate the design by building his own home in the heart of the beloved Longcommon. On October 28, 1869, Olmsted chastised Childs in a letter:

> I have just been informed that a private house is to be placed in the midst of the Long Common. I cannot express to you how much I am shocked and pained to hear that such a suggestion could for a moment be entertained. It is not a matter for argument. It sets aside at once all the study which we have given to your enterprise as of no value and breaks the plan in its most vital point. If you have the least respect for our judgment; if you think that all the study and experience we have had in matters of this kind should be regarded as of any consequence, I most earnestly beg you to abandon the plan.[41]

Childs ultimately relocated his home, but it would be the first of many challenges as to ownership and proper usage of public space. Without direct intervention from Olmsted, village residents would need to learn how to self-police. Property rights on public commons have been debated since feudal times, and this conflict would endure throughout Riverside's history.

Nature—and competitive developers—also seemed to conspire against the fledgling Riverside community. "Ague also prevails at Riverside the beautiful suburban city on the Des Plaines River and was prevalent last Summer on the Fox River throughout its full length." This headline, from the June 15, 1872, *True Republican* newspaper, added fuel to rumors that Riverside's riverine location could result in unhealthy conditions. Mosquito-borne illnesses such as ague (malaria) were greatly feared, and unscrupulous real estate

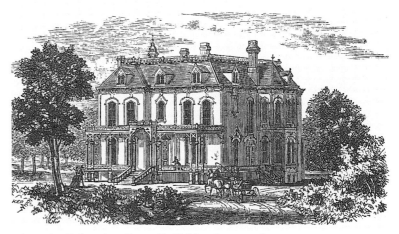

Olmsted railed against Emery E. Childs, who wanted to build his private home on the public Longcommon. Village of Riverside, Riverside Historical Commission.

developers had been known to start rumors to discourage competitive investments. The only recourse was to reiterate the message that Riverside's elevation precluded this threat. As a river valley village in the flatlands of Illinois, any kind of altitude brings bragging rights. Nearby, the self-proclaimed suburban Summit rises 610 feet above sea level, while Riverside boasts an additional 10 feet. Both communities are slightly higher than Chicago (595 feet) itself.

Financial crises, including lagging home sales, the Chicago Fire of 1871, and the national fiscal panic of 1873, ultimately resulted in the RIC bankruptcy and could have been the death knell for Riverside. Emery Childs returned to New York, and David Gage, under scrutiny and later conviction of embezzlement of Chicago treasury funds, left the state. The remaining original RIC members stayed in Riverside, and three, Leverett Murray, William Allen, and George Kimbark, joined the petition to incorporate Riverside in 1875. By election in August 1875, Carol Gaytes, an attorney and teacher, was chosen as the village's first president. Trustees included Henry Seelye, an original RIC member, George Chambers, Ezra Sherman, George Gilbert, and contractor John Cochran.

In the first four months as an operating entity, in addition to rules on governance, the newly formed board adopted twelve ordinances. This first suite of rules focused on law and order and public health. Several rules imposed restraints on animals running at large; others concerned liquor licensing, prohibition of firearms and explosives, and the establishment of a police office. These laws prioritized the tranquil and healthful aspects (untethered animals were considered vectors for disease) of Riverside along with an early rule specifically against disturbance of the peace. The first sign of stewardship for Riverside's enduring design, along with these rules promoting tranquility, were laws passed on August 17, 1875, to enact fines for "Damage to Forestry."

The board faced significant challenges. Since the RIC had dissolved two years prior, maintenance of the village had fallen behind. Responding to an inquiry from Olmsted, Louis Schermerhorn reported on the conditions in Riverside in 1877. No new homes had been built in two years, and although the roads were holding up well, the sidewalks were failing. The hotel was in ruins, and Schermerhorn opined that the depressed real estate market and unending RIC litigation slashed Riverside prices to 25–50 percent of their original value. Many of the forty-five homes in Riverside were rented at $25 per month—a far cry from their original $8,000–$12,000 purchase cost. He reported, "The borders and public grounds are fairly kept—not hairline in perfect neatness—but orderly and free from offence. The grass is kept within bounds with three cuttings during the summer & the trees pruned and protected."[42] The climate (and perhaps initial planting size) proved too treacherous for many original plantings of trees and shrubs, with 10 percent having failed.

Despite this somewhat dismal report, Schermerhorn remained optimistic, noting that the new board of trustees consisted of good stewards interested in preserving the plan. They, and Riverside residents, would be tested in the next decades.

As earlier noted, many of Olmsted's design elements (walkability, incorporation of green space, proximity to mass transit, and the like) are also goals of community planning today. Vacant land today is not as plentiful as in 1869, so urban infill projects, for example, try to incorporate green space on roofs and vertical spaces. In some "green" communities (such as Tryon Farm of Michigan City, Indiana, and Seaside in Walton County, Florida), the size of private land is greatly reduced, with dwellings more tightly clustered together. Transit-oriented development, a planning technique to curb urban sprawl, is often promoted in the United States with attractive funding grants. The goal is to offer residential housing within a half mile of mass transit to encourage public use. Today, walkability is highly desirable with some Internet home-buying sites calculating a home's walkability or bikeability score based on proximity to amenities.

NOTES FROM THE FORMATIVE YEARS

Early threats to any newly developed community often parallel those faced by the nascent Riverside: competition, financial security, and governance. Competition among new developments is ever-present as the reach of Internet advertising is significantly broader than the media used in Olmsted's day. But, like the Riverside Improvement Company, today's developers continue to rely on open-house previews with esteemed dignitaries invited. Whereas they may not hire a Pullman car to bring the city's elite for a day of horse races and card playing, high-end developers often conduct elaborate brokers' open houses to create media awareness. New developments are often risky propositions, and unsold lots deter potential buyers. Just as the RIC required purchasers to build on lots (rather than trade vacant lots in speculation), similar rules apply to lot sales today.

History records efforts where planned suburbs have failed spectacularly, particularly after the exit of their originator. Author Kenneth Jackson cites Garden City, New York, as an early planned suburb in the same league as Riverside and Llewellyn Park. Garden City, begun like Riverside in 1869, included wide roads and lot sizes, interspersed parks, and a prairie location on Long Island near commuter service to Manhattan. A speculative project by businessman A. T. Stewart and architect John Kellum, Stewart's business model offered rentals to help control the housing and restrict occupants to upper-class residents. Kellum died in 1871 and Stewart in 1876, and by the 1890s, only half the homes were occupied.[43] With all the ingredients of a Riverside, the death of the key players nonetheless doomed the suburb.

The formative years of any development are, perhaps, the most fraught with financial risk and therefore risk to the designer's plan. Even after incorporation in 1875, Riverside's village trustees could have proposed a measure to sell a grouping of unbuilt lots to another developer, thus destroying the holistic integrity of Olmsted's design. Since most of the trustees owned lots in Riverside, this apparently was not an attractive solution. Furthermore, then-unpleasant events embroiling Riverside—lawsuits and nationwide financial panics—made selling the unbuilt lots more difficult. What were then considered calamities ironically preserved the original design.

*During the Progressive Era, Riverside struggled with the effect of crowds and technology on Olmsted's design. The Hofmann Dam (at left), in neighboring Lyons,
was promoted as part of a park to draw visitors, and the bridge opened Riverside to day-trippers from surrounding picnic areas.* Photo by William Suriano.

CHAPTER 4

Progressives and Pollution (1880–1929)

The electric lights went on, newfangled phones starting ringing, and some wacky wheelmen tooled around Riverside's curvy roads. All of this upheaval occurred in Riverside during the Progressive Era in America, 1880–1929. Millions of visitors had come to Chicago's 1893 World's Fair, and many included Riverside in their itinerary. Later, the so-called socialists began picnicking next door, first drawn to nearby Forest Home Cemetery, where the Haymarket Martyrs' Monument was dedicated and associated activists were buried. The neighborhood was changing.

The Progressive Era marked a period when industrialization caused great disparity in wealth between industrialists and the swell of impoverished immigrants, and several movements were launched to improve government, the environment, and working conditions. These national efforts were prominent in Chicago, where labor unions grew strong, a prairie design ethic coexisted with environmental issues, and immigrants filled the burgeoning factory lines. World War I, women's suffrage, and the confluence of flappers, the Lost Generation, and crime in Chicago influenced communities nationwide.

These were decades of technology changes and great upheaval, when social reformers sought to neutralize wealth inequalities and protect national environmental assets—and Riverside reflected local and national movements. In Chicago, reformer Jane Addams fought for immigrant rights, and attorney Clarence Darrow defended labor unions. Theodore Roosevelt, environmentalist-in-chief, served as president of the United States from 1901 to 1909. Sometimes riding the waves of national movements and sometimes rocking the boat themselves, Riverside residents tailored the novel ideas of the various movements to the landscape of their village. New inventions, such as electricity, and even avid bicyclists powered by the novel machines, both helped and hindered efforts to keep Riverside the same—but better.

For those fifty years after 1880, the City of Chicago, then America's fastest-growing city, increased in population more than sixfold, with about 2.7 million residents in 1920.[1] While some of this growth was due to an 1889 annexation of surrounding towns, by 1890 almost 80 percent of Chicagoans were born abroad or were children of newly arrived immigrants.[2] Riverside, while not nearly as crowded as the overflowing population of Chicago, mirrored a fivefold increase in population, from about 500 residents in 1880 to 2,600 in 1920. Even as Riversiders aimed to achieve the lofty ideals of the Progressives, village residents also contended with potential realities of social change.

All but two (Henry Seelye and Alpheus Badger) of the early Riverside founders passed away in the 1880s.[3] With the fate of the village in the hands of the newly formed and elected village trustees and with nearly all RIC correspondence lost in the 1871 Chicago fire, Olmsted's original design for the community became a cipher forever open to interpretation by current and future generations.

As Olmsted once predicted, committees charged with "improving" village designs often gilded the lily. Many of these improvement groups derived from the City Beautiful movement, itself an outgrowth of the World's Columbian Exposition in Chicago. In an article published posthumously, Olmsted recalled a simple town square that was overimproved with extra sidewalks, monuments, and gardenesque flowers: "It would seem to have been thought by most of those who directly or indirectly lead village improvements that a choice of beauty is mainly a choice of embellishments." Instead, he offered this guiding advice: "Time, effort, and money expended on embellishments, without painstaking thought as to their ultimate result, are apt to be worse than wasted; while wise forethought as to purposes and tendencies may so shape the simplest utilitarian necessities of a village as to give it the beauty of consistency, harmony and truth."[4] In this Progressive Era where "beautification" committees and garden clubs flourished, Riverside became vulnerable to this excess of embellishment.

PUBLIC PARKS: "THE PART COLORED GREEN REPRESENTED PUBLIC PROPERTY"

As promised in his *Preliminary Report* to the RIC, Olmsted reserved some of the best land, along the river and in wooded groves throughout the village, as public parks to encourage a love of nature and social gatherings. But the prime location of these parks sparked greed in some people, such as Emery Childs, whose desired homesite usurped public space. The temptation to commandeer land would return again and again over time: the parks and commons were coveted for personal use, and bits and pieces of the greenswards were subject to squatters or outright misappropriation.

Such was the threat in 1885 when Henry and Lucy Glos leased land to Henry Braun for cattle pasturage near Indian Garden (also colloquially called "Gardens" by both residents and news accounts) and the river. The Gloses claimed to have bought the property, about fifty-five acres, as part of a tax sale in 1881. The village argued that that land could never have been taxed because it was public property. Therein lay the rub. Public spaces on the original plan of Riverside were colored green. Subsequent maps, drawn after the Chicago fire, lacked color and therefore the commonly accepted definition of public versus private land.[5] For the want of a colored pencil, the land grab was on.

On September 17, 1885, the village brought suit against Glos and others in the circuit court. The suit was decided in favor of the village in 1887 with the decree noting that the general understanding of the public, buyers and sellers of property, and the Riverside Improvement Company was that the original green-colored parcels were public.[6] Strengthening the court victory, in October 1888 the village passed an ordinance prohibiting any private structures to be built on public parkways.

Undeterred by the ordinance, Riverside resident and coal dealer Patrick Ronan challenged the rule by operating an icehouse on the riverbank just south of the train tracks. For decades, the Ronans had lived in Riverside and farmed the land prior to 1870. Once again, the village sued and prevailed, asserting that the land was public. In 1893, in an unrelated lawsuit, a definition of public versus private space emerged. Among the witnesses, William Le Baron Jenney testified in a deposition as to the original coloring legends on Olmsted's plan:

Q. I will ask you what, if anything, you know about the meaning or significance, of the parts colored on this map?

A. That was intended as public property, not roads, that is property that was either lawns or borders.

Q. Did you ever hear any statements made by the officers of the Riverside Improvement Company as to the significance of this coloring?

A. Oh it was well and universally understood among us all that this property, the part colored green[,] represented public property, not roads.[7]

In yet another court case, settled in 1894, the Village of Riverside ceded more than ninety acres of public parkland along the Des Plaines River to one Charles L. Colby in exchange for ownership of the waterworks. Through some previous real estate deals, Colby seemingly legitimately laid claim to the critical infrastructure of the village.[8] The tables turned again at the turn of the century, when the village set its sights on a park space. Near the same land sought earlier by Ronan, the village attempted to build a road across the railroad tracks from Forest Avenue to Bloomingbank Road, but neighbors opposed. Resident George A. Maclean and others sought an injunction against the village, saying the road would adversely affect their private property values. This seminal court case rose to the Illinois Supreme Court in 1903, which upheld a lower court's decision that the village could not build the road. The village argued that Olmsted's original map showed a road along the river and that the extension of West Avenue would serve this purpose as a pleasure drive. The court sharply disagreed:

There is nothing to show that West Avenue, if extended across this park, would be restricted, in the use to be made of it, to a mere pleasure driveway. The evidence shows that, under some arrangement between the village and the railroad company, the grade where this crossing is to be made will be raised between

Riverside's abundant greenspace attracted many proposals for private use. Photo by Twenty Seven and a Half photography.

4 and 5 feet above the level of the park. An unsightly, elevated roadway will thus be created through what has been a park, planted with trees and shrubs, and cared for as such. It is not to be supposed that persons driving for pleasure would attempt to drive a distance of 135 feet, more or less, up or down an inclined plane, and over a complicated and dangerous railroad.[9]

With the deciding of this case, attempts to usurp public parks settled for a while. The Riverside case proved precedent for other important court decisions in Illinois, such as in Aaron Montgomery Ward's storied battle to save Chicago's lakefront park. In this dispute between Ward and the City of Chicago, he famously quoted the words written on an early Chicago map, "forever open free and clear," to argue that the lakefront should be free of buildings and obstructions. The court's decision in favor of Ward has curtailed attempts in Chicago to build on public land ever since.

Olmsted specified "artificial improvements" such as gas lamps to bring city amenities to Riverside. They remain today. Photo by author.

More than 27 million visitors came to Chicago to attend the renowned 1893 World's Columbian Exposition. The fair had been years in the making, with Frederick Law Olmsted returning to Chicago to design the fairgrounds in Jackson Park. Riverside, like many nearby neighborhoods, enjoyed the uptick in business related to the fair. Riverside residents and businessmen made plans for a new hotel and boardinghouses to host visitors. J. J. Reynolds, local Riverside greenhouse owner, was considered by the Exposition Board of Managers for the role of chief of the horticulture department.[10]

Beyond these immediate effects, the 1893 World's Fair directly influenced Riverside's growth, residents' attitudes toward visitors, and use of public space. The landscape styles at the fair, from Olmsted's naturalistic Wooded Island to the exotic specimens in the Horticultural Palace, inspired American gardening taste, including in Riverside. Inventions and technology filtered from the fairgrounds to individual front yards and backyards. The World's Fair launched the nationwide City Beautiful urban planning ideal, and Riverside felt its effects.

Electricity: "Unsightly Cedar Poles"

Lighting at world's fairs promised spectacular displays and exhibitions of progress in this burgeoning field. Five thousand lights, then considered a marvel, had illuminated the Main Building at the World Cotton Centennial Exposition in New Orleans in 1884. Less than ten years later, with electricity becoming more prevalent, the massive Electricity Building at the World's Columbian Exposition dedicated space to inventions in electricity from around the world.

Riverside had been flirting with electricity since 1891, when a village ordinance gave approval for Riverside Edison Company to build an electric plant on the riverbank. Almost immediately, the fledgling power company ran into trouble. Riverside trustees brought legal action against the company for erecting "unsightly cedar poles."[11] Here was an early example of village officials prioritizing Olmsted's aesthetic over technological progress. Once design standards were agreed upon in 1893, the village reinstated the franchise.

Olmsted had included gas lighting, then the foremost advancement in lighting, in his specifications for Riverside. Lighting was considered a common improvement for cities but not for rural areas. As technical advances continued through the 1920s, the Riverside Village Board considered replacing the gas lamps with electricity throughout the village. Some residents favored the move, particularly when lurid reporting about a murder in suburban Evanston raised fears of darkened streets.[12] After nearly a decade of debate over gas versus electricity, the Great Depression finally delivered the verdict for the cheaper option. The board signed a renewal for gas lighting in 1930, thus averting a major change to Riverside's historic charm. Gas is still used to power the flames in most of Riverside's streetlights. Although Chicago's bright lights spill over into Riverside's night sky, the village's quaint gas lights do not greatly contribute to light pollution even today.

The telephone reached Riverside in 1894. Disappointed once by ugly poles, the village board required that the Chicago Telephone Company provide "first class, straight and symmetrical cedar poles" that "shall be painted olive green."[13] Both franchises, for electricity and the telephone, were strongly encouraged to bury their cables and lines and use poles only where explicitly approved by the board of trustees. The ordinance expressly prohibited tree trimming for pole installation unless absolutely necessary, and

Riverside featured prominently in popular trips from the city, especially as streetcars made the journey affordable. Here, one of the few straight streets in Riverside features a shelter and median of trees and grass where once ran trolleys. Photo by author.

then only under the direction of the village commissioner of public works or "expert men furnished by the Chicago Telephone Company."[14] The village thus achieved progress without compromising the aesthetics of the naturalistic beauty of Riverside. Today, it is extremely rare to see telephone poles, except between backyards along the easements.

Electrified streetcars greatly affected Riverside. Obtaining the franchise for a railroad right of way became an aggressively competitive business in the Chicago area with figures such as Samuel Insull and Charles Yerkes achieving notoriety. This discord extended into the suburbs where new tracks were being laid. In Riverside, a bitterly contested election for the village board split candidates between those favoring the Suburban Electric Road and those favoring the Ogden Electric Road.[15] The Suburban line won the franchise, although it was bought out several years later.

The new streetcar extended west down Twenty-Sixth Street to Des Plaines Avenue, where it turned south through Riverside. This Suburban line connected to the broader electric rail system such that, via transfers, a rider could thereby travel to virtually all points of the city. Traveling to or from Chicago, commuters now had more frequent and less expensive options than the CB&Q Railroad. While convenient for Riverside residents, the streetcars brought more traffic to the tiny village.

Would the rural nature of Riverside be threatened by this invasion of technology? By 1912, the *Chicago Tribune* opined that the demarcation between city and suburbs began west of the Des Plaines River—that is, beyond Riverside. "The country between the Desplaines [sic] River [which includes Riverside] and the city limits of Chicago is now so tapped and girdled by steam and electric transportation that people living in that district are now practically in Chicago."[16] Riverside had enjoyed growth in recent years, the *Tribune* noted, and an "unbroken chain of villages" extended between the city and Olmsted's suburb. The Burlington railroad razed its roundhouse at Riverside, no longer using it as its terminal, and extended more suburban stops to Aurora.[17]

Riversiders favored the opening of Harlem Avenue to the Chicago and West Towns Railway. An ordinance was passed in 1913 to grant the franchise. Property owners felt this new electric line would open up entrances to the east side of the village and thus encourage development of that part of town. The new railway would also, it was hoped, divert traffic, in particular from picnic crowds west of Riverside.[18]

Electrification of home appliances came piecemeal to Riverside homes. Early Riverside resident Robert Uhlich recalled a wood-coal kitchen stove and deliveries from the iceman and milkman in the 1920s. Only later did his family buy a "General Electric refrigerator with the compressor mounted in a round housing on the top of the refrigerator."[19] Charles Osberg, who reputedly came from Thomas Edison's Menlo laboratory to help install electricity at the World's Columbian Exposition, ultimately set up an appliance shop in the 1920s in Riverside's downtown district.[20] Electricity made many aspects of Riverside life easier, but would the love of the outdoors diminish as indoor life became more comfortable?

New Visitors: "Crowds That Came to the River Were Also Attracting Pickpockets"

Progressivism, as espoused by Chicago's Jane Addams, included extending a helping hand to immigrants. Her Hull House on Chicago's West Side offered many programs to expose the urban poor to the outdoors. This she did through philanthropic efforts such as the Bowen Club, a summer camp near Waukegan, Illinois, and also by encouraging Hull House residents and neighbors to board the streetcar and enjoy picnics and the outdoors in the outlying suburbs.

Riverside became a prime destination, since its paved streets and sidewalks and grassy banks lining the river offered nature, civilized. Riverside had also been surrounded by well-known picnic areas along the Des Plaines River to the west and south. These groves, privately owned, were rented out to political, ethnic, labor, religious, and other groups, as well as to families seeking a Sunday outing. "Kimbark's Woods," in the unincorporated northwest portion of Riverside, Haase's Grove, Reissig's Grove, and Bergman's Grove all hosted picnic parties of various sizes and denominations. The nearby cemeteries, Forest Home and Waldheim, north of Riverside, attracted funeral parties and visits. When the Haymarket agitators (labor activists, anarchists, or martyrs, depending on one's view at the time, who were vilified for inciting the 1886 Haymarket Riot) were buried in Forest Home after the 1889 uprising in Chicago, members of the Socialist Party frequented the monument there and also nearby groves.[21] A dedication ceremony in 1893 for the Haymarket monument in Forest Home drew thousands of visitors.

This popularity proved a double-edged sword for Riverside. The village board voted to proscribe any boat landings that provided livery services on public property along the riverbanks. The local newspaper noted that "the river was a mecca for all classes of Chicago folks, both desirable and undesirable[,] and that the crowds that came to the river were also attracting pickpockets. The electric cars have been worked steadily between Riverside and Chicago by pickpockets for the past two years."[22]

On the fringes of Riverside, itinerant camps, from all ethnic backgrounds, sprang up with tents sheltering fortune tellers and clairvoyants. Many of Chicago's immigrant populations rode streetcars to these encampments to discern the future and to collect roots and leaves of plants as had been used in the Old Country for home remedies or food. Between 1907 and 1908, a forty-five-acre amusement park built along the Des Plaines River on Ogden Avenue in nearby Lyons featured a recreation of "Old Bohemia" with dancers, acrobats, and shops. Neighboring towns, including Riverside, voiced concerns over the business. One minister from La Grange pronounced it "merely a cloak under which it acts as a feeder to the white slave trade of the Chicago red light district."[23]

Crowds in the picnic areas also wreaked havoc on the natural beauty of the riverbanks, according to one writer for the local *Riverside News.* "The natural beauties along the river are fast being destroyed. When Riverside was first laid out, there were more kinds of wild flowers to be found in our woods than in the same area anywhere in this part of the county. Nothing could have been more beautiful than the strip of woodland along the river from the mill bridge to the cemeteries." The writer decried the vandalism done to

Field trips sponsored by the University of Chicago botany department, such as this one ca. 1921, allowed participants to explore Riverside for its natural beauty. University of Chicago Photographic Archive, [apf8.01588], Hanna Holborn Gray Special Collections Research Center, University of Chicago Library.

Riverside became known as a place for city dwellers to picnic. Chicago History Museum, ICHi.183246A.

Fishing, as shown in this hand-colored vintage view, became so popular with out-of-towners that Riverside banned it. Author's collection.

The Prairie Club of Chicago, an early environmental group, hosted one of its first hikes in Riverside. Here, club members clamber over barbed wire, ca. 1908. Courtesy of Prairie Club Archives, Westchester Township History Museum, Chesterton, Ind.

trees from picnic fires in the groves, asking, "Why must we allow countless hordes of fishermen and merry-makers utterly to disregard the interests of the future?"[24]

In 1902, the Riverside Village Board of Trustees enacted an ordinance to prohibit fishing within the village.[25] This draconian measure, meant to discourage loiterers, applied to residents as well, thus creating self-inflicted punishments. The fishing prohibition, with many revisions, finally was removed from the books in 2017, when it became apparent that other rules forbidding alcohol and rowdy noise secured the actual desired results.

CONSERVATION IN RIVERSIDE: "WE WANT EVERYONE TO ENJOY OUR FLOWERS"

The forests near Riverside became increasingly valuable as natural areas succumbed to ever-expanding development radiating from Chicago. Julius Rosenwald, philanthropist and millionaire, gave $50,000 toward building a clubhouse for Chicago schoolteachers and social workers.[26] The remaining tracts of forested land west of the Des Plaines River beckoned developers, with projects ranging from social programs to amusement parks.

Consistent with national Progressive early environmental efforts, groups formed in Chicago to bring awareness to and help protect rapidly dwindling natural areas. One such group, the Prairie Club of Chicago, sponsored hikes around Chicago's unspoiled natural areas. Founded in 1908 by famed landscape architect Jens Jensen, the Prairie Club often chose Riverside as its destination. The hikers, mainly schoolteachers and other education professionals, strode along Riverside's riverbank with their hiking boots and long skirts, suitcoats, and ties.

Wishing to protect the natural plantings, Riverside women formed a chapter of the Wildflower Preservation Society in 1914.

The group, like its national umbrella organization, sought to educate the public about native flowers and the importance of keeping them in situ. Riversiders had noted that native flowers were disappearing from the riverbank woods. Announcing the formation of the new society, a local newspaper observed with dismay, "Crowds of people from the city and our own people carry away baskets full of withered flowers and roots. We want everyone to enjoy our flowers . . . that everyone may enjoy them for years to come."[27]

The group was headed by Catharine Mitchell, a Smith College graduate, Riverside resident on Fairbank Road, and a luminary in national conservation circles. Mitchell served as secretary of Chicago's Conservation Council and the Illinois Audubon Society and in leadership positions in other nature-related groups.[28] In its first year with some forty members and nearly thirty junior members, the Riverside chapter of the Wildflower Preservation Society helped schoolchildren plant white violets in Riverside, conducted four field trips, and participated in lectures on the Indiana Dunes by such well-known conservationists as Dr. H. C. Cowles.

Along with Catharine Mitchell, membership in Jensen's other conservation group, the Friends of Our Native Landscape, included Avery and Queene Ferry Coonley, Riverside residents who built a large Frank Lloyd Wright–designed estate in 1907. Dwight H. Perkins, who led many Prairie Club walks, preceded Wright by designing an 1893 Riverside home, one of his first commissions as a solo architect. Jens Jensen further espoused conservationist ideals for Riverside in his native plant landscape designs for the Coonley estate and, in the same time frame, for the 1907 Louis Sullivan–designed Babson estate.

Perkins was instrumental in developing many green spaces in and around Chicago. Besides offering outdoor exercise and fun, the purpose of the Prairie Club hikes, which were open to the public, was to expose Chicago-area residents to the beauty of their natural surroundings. The 1909 Plan of Chicago, spearheaded by Daniel Burnham, which grew out of the 1893 World's Fair City Beautiful movement, included generous green space in new parks and boulevards. In tandem with this, the City of Chicago hired Dwight Perkins to lead a Special Park Commission, a blue-ribbon panel of leading Chicago businessmen and philanthropists, plus landscape architects Jens Jensen and O. C. Simonds. The commission was to identify needs for green space and propose land that could be obtained for the public good. The report recommended 8,000 acres in the Des Plaines River valley.[29] Earlier, in 1903, the Cook County Board authorized an Outer Belt Commission, whose board included Burnham and Perkins. Perkins recommended that, with their similar aims, both groups be consolidated into a "Commission for the Creation of an Outer Belt of Parks and Boulevards for the County of Cook and the City of Chicago."[30] This commission would form the organizational precedent for the Forest Preserve District of Cook County.

Here, then, for Riverside, was a possible solution for addressing the unruly crowds that spilled into the village from the nearby woods and groves. Would the creation of a forest preserve system, including lands surrounding Riverside, help police the crowds that descended on Riverside, or would it encourage even more visitors and vandalism? With great interest, Riversiders watched the multi-year effort to create the forest preserves.

An editorial in the *Riverside News* expressed favor for the forest preserves, noting, "On any pleasant summer day many weary flat dwellers and others of Chicago can be found enjoying pleasures afforded by these natural beauties, and as a rule the frequenters of these forests are of the best and most substantial citizens and are singularly free from the rowdy class. . . . These woods are the reverse of the amusement parks and beer gardens and justly claim and secure a different class of patrons."[31]

As can be imagined, with the multiplicity of landowners, municipalities, and diverging interests, establishing the forest preserves became an extraordinary balancing act of conservation versus development. Between 1904 and 1913, the Illinois state legislature passed three different Forest Preserve Acts; finally in 1915, Cook County officially created the forest preserves.[32] In one of the initial scouting missions, a delegation of state legislators and City of Chicago Park officials explored many areas, and "the territory near Riverside along the Desplaines river was the first visited."[33] Often accompanying these scouting groups was George Hofmann, from neighboring Lyons, who hosted lunches for the group.

Local Riversider and environmentalist Catharine Mitchell created postcards of wildflowers like this trillium found in Riverside. Author's collection.

Hofmann had been buying property along the Des Plaines with the intent to build a series of amusement parks.

The western fringes of forests encircling Riverside drew visitors especially on Sundays, the solitary day of rest for most Chicago-based immigrant laborers. "Riverside was hemmed in largely by picnic groves, which in reality were beer gardens that extended in an almost unbroken line from along Ogden Avenue in Lyons to Des Plaines Avenue in what is now North Riverside," the *Riverside News* reported.[34] The picnic groves were unregulated, and crowds boarded trolley cars for a full day of beer-fueled merriment. Their return to the city often included boisterous and bombastic forays into Riverside.

The *Riverside News* editorialized in 1912, "It is not necessary nor desirable that outsiders shall be deprived of enjoying anything and everything but they should not be allowed to destroy anything. If it is not within our power to police and protect our property and they persist in destruction there seems to be but one course and that is to keep strangers out until we can admit them under proper conditions."[35]

By 1918, much of the area along the river from the railroad tracks north to about Twenty-Sixth Street had been acquired, along with patches around Salt Creek and areas along the river in Lyons.[36] The forest preserves ultimately provided that wooded buffer on the west side of the river that Olmsted included in his General Plan. As Cook County public property, however, all control over the use, maintenance, and rules controlling the land was ceded.

With conservation walks, Wildflower Preservation Society efforts, and other local ecological campaigns, Riversiders became more interested in native plantings. Catharine Mitchell prepared colored postcards of native plants to help educate residents and the general populace on the benefits and beauties of native flora and fauna.

SHARING THE RIVER: "THE POOL ABOVE THE RIVERSIDE DAM WAS A SEETHING SEPTIC TANK"

In his *Preliminary Report* to the RIC, Olmsted commented on the purity of the Des Plaines River: "The water of the river is said to be ordinarily very clear, and we found it tolerably so after a heavy rain, which is remarkable in a prairie stream. It abounds with fish and wild fowl, is adapted to pleasure-boating, and can be improved in this respect. In parts, it already presents much beauty, and is everywhere susceptible of being refined and enriched by art to a degree which will render it altogether charming."[37] But what a difference several decades made: the once-beautiful river now suffered from pollution and flooding.

Riverside, at the mercy of upstream discharges, could not control this shared natural resource by village ordinance; it needed cooperation from neighboring towns whose growth burgeoned. Comparing the prior two decades, a 1901 report on sanitary conditions explained, "It will be noted that the greatest increase of urban population has been upon the Des Plaines Valley, which is adjacent to the city of Chicago. The urban population in this case having increased 43.3 per cent, the rural population 5 percent, and the total population 23.8 percent."[38]

Once a swampland, the Chicago area had a long history with legislation covering drainage and flooding. The same year that Riverside was designed, verbiage was added to the Illinois Constitution: "The General Assembly may pass laws permitting the owners or occupants of lands to construct drains and ditches for agricultural and sanitary purposes, across the lands of others."[39] Several statewide legislative acts attempted to control floods and pollution in the last quarter of the nineteenth century. The 1879 Illinois Farm Drainage Act regulated subsurface tiling and open ditches.

In 1889, the Illinois legislature created the Sanitary District of Chicago, whose purview included the Des Plaines River.

Flooding due to burgeoning populations and development of natural wetlands plagued the Riverside area particularly in spring. Other seasons brought severe pollution problems. According to a Chicago Sanitary District report, "During the summer of 1910 in the upper river the pool above the Riverside dam was a seething septic tank."[40] Water was so stagnant that nothing flowed over the dam.

Riversiders' patience with the intolerable river conditions wore thin by 1912. At a mass meeting of truculent villagers, the "Des Plaines River Committee" was formed to file suits against the alleged offending municipalities of Maywood, Forest Park, River Forest, and Melrose Park. The committee hired drainage expert Langdon Pearse and attorney Amos C. Miller to document conditions through photographs and interviews of people along the riverbank. The Rivers and Lakes Commission of Illinois joined the suit as a party complainant. The committee reported in October 1914, "Just as our main case was about to be tried, the Sanitary District of Chicago sent an attorney to appear before the Court and to ask that the trial be postponed ninety days."[41]

The judge agreed to the delay, during which time the Sanitary District promised to rectify the situation. The Sanitary District provided particularly damning information about the river in its 1914 report, noting, "The principal source of complaint in the past four or five years [has] been Riverside. . . . The conditions complained of at Riverside have been general nuisance, masses of dying or dead fish, and the general unfitness of the stream at times for any pleasure purpose. Odors have been noted by residents even as far away as a quarter of a mile along the entire frontage. At times conditions have been almost intolerable for the people residing immediately along the bank of the river."[42]

A dam on the river has been rebuilt many times. Dams and upstream pollution caused water quality issues for the Des Plaines River near Riverside. Author's collection.

The Sanitary District report proposed a number of remedies, including channel dredging, better screens for solids, and new and better sewage intercepts. So convincingly had Riverside made its case that the report devoted a special appendix to Riverside issues. Some excerpts:

The general condition of the river is inimical to fish life. . . . As a source of drinking water the Des Plaines at Riverside is absolutely unsafe. . . . Owing to the high content of organic matter, at times, and products of decomposition, the water would seem undesirable as a source for boiler use. . . . It is said that the locomotive engineers on the C. B. & Q. will only use the water in emergency. . . . Ice cut from the pond above the Riverside dam is undesirable for household use. . . . The nuisance at the upper end has disfigured the river for park purposes, soiling the banks, and spreading odors. At Riverside, the character of the river has been injured for park purposes by the deposits of sludge, washed down from above, as well as by the odors on the water and in the air. . . . The nuisance, even the intermittent, is a detriment to property fronting or adjoining the river.[43]

Progress came slowly in cleaning up the river, and the village was forced to sue a number of times as the waterway continued to be plagued by ever-expanding populations and the additional pollution caused. River pollution was and is an ongoing threat to Riverside.

AUTOMOBILES CHANGE THE LANDSCAPE: "THE HIGH SEPARATE CURB WAS NOT ATTRACTIVE"

Riverside's well-maintained roads again lured visitors in the 1910s and 1920s. Automobiles driven by tastemakers and free spirits made their debut in the village. One motor enthusiast noted, "No matter what direction you come from, you can always tell the moment you strike the Riverside boundary. It is a great pleasure to ride throughout the village. . . . Other suburbs would take a few lessons in road making."[44]

Automobile clubs targeted Riverside as their destination. Members of the Chicago Auto Club made Riverside their first day trip of the year in April 1904. By 1914, more clubs and individual riders flocked to the village, sometimes causing havoc. The local paper reported, "Riverside police arrested eight young men and women for 'joy riding' through Riverside on a Sunday morning. Fined a dollar each, the youngsters spent some time in jail but were released in time for breakfast."[45]

As early as 1913, Riverside received acclaim in *Concrete Highway Magazine* for the newly paved concrete roads. Concrete won over several other materials as being sturdier than the original

Horses, outfitted with phaetons as shown here, were ultimately replaced by automobiles. Olmsted's curving roads discouraged fast speed. Author's collection.

Riverside's Public Works Department extolled the virtues of concrete pavement for automobiles in 1920. Concrete Highway Magazine, January 1920.

macadam, which suffered under the increased traffic and weight. F. C. Seibert, village superintendent, who authored the self-congratulatory article, noted that "most of Riverside's pavement has a low four-inch integral curb on each side. It was believed that the high separate curb was not attractive, was not a necessity, and more costly than the integral curb built as a monolith with the pavement. This type of construction has proved entirely practical, economical and attractive."[46]

But with the addition of concrete roads and curbs—while they were perhaps more practical than macadam—a little bit of Riverside design was lost. Concrete stands out starkly against the green landscape more than would the more natural look of the crushed stone macadam. Cobblestone gutters, charming in Olmsted's design, also succumbed to the new road technology.

Automobiles required new road materials and also challenged the signature road layout. By the 1920s, sufficient automobile traffic cruised through Riverside that safety became an issue. The *Riverside News* printed a graphic and accompanying proposal by local real estate agent Henry Miller on how to change the roads near the water tower to reduce accidents. "Cut off a point of the triangular park southeast of the school," it began, also recommending better alignment of the sidewalks and widening of streets.[47] This suggestion was one of many to this main five-way intersection in the middle of town.

The automobile not only challenged Riverside's public ways but also reworked private grounds. Initially, wealthy homeowners, first adopters of the automobile, converted stables and coach houses to garages. Little else was necessary—the expansive grounds of such residences typically included a turnaround near the stables so that a horse, and then an automobile, could orient itself to point toward the street. Architects of smaller homes, the bungalows and Craftsman-style residences built in the Progressive Era, tended to construct detached garages at the back of the property, connected to the street by a straight driveway. This necessitated driving a car in reverse and thus backing out of a driveway, which put drivers on a literal collision course with pedestrians on the sidewalk. (By 1935, automobile owners and pedestrians were pitted against each other in the matter of overhanging shrubs on sidewalks. Mailmen began complaining about the dripping branches after rains, but homeowners with cars protested against shrubbery trimming.)[48]

GARDENS AND LANDSCAPE: "REISSIG'S EXOTIC GARDENS"

Private gardens, which in Olmsted's design were supposed to meld into the public landscape, underwent changes reflecting national and regional trends. The Progressive Era's famed City Beautiful movement, which married green space and urban elements as in Riverside, received significant impetus from the World's Columbian Exposition. Olmsted's landscape for that fair, as it complemented Daniel Burnham's architecture and artwork like that of Augustus Saint-Gaudens, is often credited with launching the green aspects of the City Beautiful movement, an urban planning effort that aimed to blend Progressive reforms with architectural and landscape beautification. Yet, even as Olmsted enjoyed his designed naturalistic effects at the fair's Wooded Island (an offset to the overall Beaux Arts style of the fair), the commercial interests of florists and growers entranced the general public.[49] The Horticultural Palace (built by Olmsted's colleague William Le Baron Jenney) dazzled with multi-hued displays of exotic flowering plants. On the fairgrounds, horticulturists and nurserymen vied for prime space to showcase their latest gaudy cultivars.

Although Olmsted and his peers had made inroads against showy plantings, there were apologists for colorful blooms. This unabashed and defiant letter from self-described "Simple Simon" to the editor of *Garden and Forest* journal in the 1880s, for example, evoked the timeless frustration of those who felt patronized by garden critics:

> Sir. I am a vulgarian. I like pretty plants. I also like to own them. I like to see them growing on my little grounds. I also like them just as much if they come from far away as if they were first found near at hand; and if they are very unlike what all my neighbors have, I love my pretty plants all the better for that. . . . To my low taste it isn't the end of all perfection in planting to secure "repose" or general sleepiness or so refined a commonplace that nobody will notice whether anything is growing near my house. I rebel against Mr. Olmsted and you and only a revolt will ease my mind and temper when you go to laying down those austere rules of landscape gardening. What! May some high artist come along and order out of the ground my pluming Pampas Grass and striped Eulalias, my delicious Japanese Maples, and the Paulownia[?] . . . Shall he make me believe that all the people who look over my fence as they go by and say this lawn is the neatest thing in the neighborhood lack good taste for admiring a plain man's collection[?] . . . Some sense ought to be shown in putting colors together but green is not the only color worth looking at in trees by vulgar eyes. . . . Make your high class parks as prim and plain as you will, but pardon common folks for putting pretty things where they can see them grow and where they can be proud of them.[50]

Garden and Forest journal, started by Olmsted friend and founding director of Harvard's Arnold Arboretum Charles Sprague Sargent, reflected the controversy of the times between exotic plant fanciers and naturalistic garden advocates. In that era, the argument mostly raged among professional landscape gardeners and wealthy estate owners. Everyday people of the Industrial Age did not concern themselves with such esoteric thoughts. They simply planted what they liked and could readily obtain.

The World's Columbian Exposition coincided with the heyday of chromolithography, wisely leveraged by seedsmen and nursery catalogs displaying exquisite images of colorful flowers. Riversiders were not immune. Some homeowners fancied geometric cutouts of annual beds in their lawns. With its extensive greenhouses in Western Springs, just a few miles west of Riverside, Vaughan's Nursery regularly advertised its seed and lawn fertilizer in the local *Riverside News*.

Within Riverside, two regionally known growers supplied gardeners with plants. The Reissig family moved from Chicago in 1872 and established their home on sixteen acres in today's North Riverside. Charles Reissig "enjoyed raising orchids and growing imported plants and earned a reputation for being an excellent grower of rare species," according to the *Riverside News*.[51] His sprawling grounds, with ten greenhouses, were known as "Reissig's Exotic Gardens," which gives an indication of the type of plant material offered and also likely planted in Riverside's home gardens. Plants could additionally be obtained through Riverside's own James D. Raynolds, a rose grower, who worked with the RIC for about a year and then bought land in Riverside. A. Schmidt also maintained greenhouses for his business on Cowley Road in the village.

Large estates, such as that of the William T. Allen house on Riverside Road, covered nearly the entire block with orchards, extensive gardens, and peacocks strutting on the grounds. Such large estates demanded the services of professional gardeners. The 1880 census listed four such gardeners who owned homes in Riverside and one individual who boarded and styled himself an "agriculturist." Three of the gardeners were born in Germany and one hailed from England, thus lending some European traditions to many of the major properties. Full-time gardeners were essential

The grounds of Robert Somerville's home, ca. 1896, show the owner's preference for geometric shapes and exotic plants rather than the naturalistic style espoused by Olmsted. Village of Riverside, Riverside Historical Commission.

A 1909 real estate ad for half-acre properties in Riverside's Third Division exhorted prospects, "Don't miss the opportunity of owning a home in the country with its beautiful scenery and pure, fresh air and the advantage of owning your own chickens and cow and raising your own vegetables."[53] All this for $225.

In 1904, the Riverside Olmsted Association (not to be confused with the later Olmsted Society), which, according to the *Chicago Tribune*, included nearly everyone in the village, sponsored an exhibition of modern architects for not only home designs but also improved grounds. The Olmsted Association's mission focused on village beautification. Invited exhibitors included then-emerging Prairie-style or Arts and Crafts architects George Maher, Howard Van Doren Shaw, Pond and Pond, and Hugh Garden of Chicago. Out-of-state architects included Pennsylvania's landscape architect J. Wilkinson Elliott, a creative nurseryman and designer; architects Wheelwright and Haven of Boston; Philadelphia's Wilson Eyre, known for innovative Shingle-style homes; and Coolidge and Carson of Boston. Some homeowners of this period chose "kit" homes, such as the famous Sears kit homes. Building the home could involve architects, contractors, or the homeowners themselves. (Curiously, local architect G. W. Ashby of the Radford Architectural Company removed his exhibit and exhorted friends to boycott the exhibition. The Radford Company produced catalogs of designs that could be constructed by homeowners themselves, purportedly saving an architect's fees.) If homeowners chose uninspired gardens, it was not for lack of exposure to classic or refined designs.

Riverside home gardens remained largely traditional despite Prairie-style influences in new Riverside architecture, and even with Jens Jensen's designs for the Coonley and Babson estates. Tastes reflected the move toward perennial gardens as espoused by English garden writer and designer Gertrude Jeykll and American

to maintaining the properties in the growing season since many wealthy homeowners summered away from Riverside.

While some homeowners' tastes ran to showy plantings, others chose simplified lawns with a smattering of trees and shrubs, as seen in photographs from the 1880–90 time frame. By the early twentieth century, however, large estates in Riverside maintained by full-time gardeners were the exception. Smaller lots became available with new subdivisions within Riverside created from parcels adjacent to but not owned by the original RIC. With many of the larger, older homes vacant due to changes in ownership, the village passed ordinances to prohibit commercial uses of the structures (such as private schools and boardinghouses).[52]

contemporaries such as Louisa King. Women garden writers began to dominate the garden style pages of popular magazines such as *Ladies' Home Journal*, which, in 1903, reached 1 million subscribers.

The Riverside Garden Club formed in 1921. Meetings, held in Riverside women's homes, focused on home beautification and also conservation. Members, following a tradition from Riverside residents associated with the Chicago Flower Mission in the 1800s, donated flowers from their gardens to Cook County Hospital and others in need.[54] The club hosted garden walks open to other suburban garden club members. As with many women's garden clubs of the era, membership required a sponsor, and an aura of exclusivity prevailed.

Perhaps in response, an alternative "Garden Lovers Club" was established in 1928 as "the new garden organization of the village to be held outside a private home."[55] Organized by Dr. Owen Rea, prizewinner in a 1927 *Chicago Tribune* garden contest, the coed club, with about forty members, was then unusual in its inclusion of men. The Rea garden, on Maplewood, contained several ponds and water features, including the backdrop of the Des Plaines River. The Garden Lovers Club focused on designs for smaller properties, as well as on overall horticultural advice.

The types of gardens in the 1920s included rock gardens and a new experimentation with ponds. The latter became popular with new concrete possibilities. Popular annuals included zinnias, larkspurs, asters, sweet alyssums, lobelia, German stock, and sweet peas. Nasturtiums fell out of favor because of insect problems. Gardeners favored such old-fashioned perennials as coreopsis, gaillardias, delphiniums, digitalis, Canterbury bells, aquilegias, Shasta daisies, chrysanthemums, phloxes, irises, and hardy lilies.[56]

Typical was the vegetable and flower garden of the Uhlich family on Downing Road. "My father was proud of his large garden. He had row upon row of grape vines. A large area was planted in corn, tomatoes, lettuce, peas, beans, cucumbers, carrots, radishes and asparagus. Currant bushes produced an ample source of jelly. . . . There were roses, hollyhocks, lilacs, dahlias, and a myriad others."[57] The Uhlich family canned the harvest and also made wine from the grapes.

Riversiders must have derived some enjoyment in gardening, because they didn't *need* to plant their own vegetables. The village's long-standing grocery store, A. R. Owen & Co., stocked a good supply of fresh fruits and vegetables, even out of season. In May, for example, patrons could purchase a quart of strawberries for ten cents, large pineapples for fifteen cents, Winesap apples at seventy-five cents per peck, a bunch of asparagus ("very large and fancy") at fifteen cents per bunch, or large-leaf lettuce for five cents.[58]

PUBLIC LANDSCAPE: DANDELIONS AND ZONING

Riverside's public landscape came under the purview of the newly created Public Improvements Committee, established by ordinance in 1900, and later under the oversight of the Parks and Roads Committee, with members appointed annually. In the early 1900s, concerns grew about weeds in the public areas, with the first weed ordinance passed in 1915. Some solutions, including one proposed by Avery Coonley, recommended hiring residents of Chicago's settlement houses to remove dandelions by hand. (Coonley himself, affiliated with Gads Hill settlement house, provided such employment for Gads Hill workers on his own estate.)[59]

The natural areas along the river, a main attraction for hikers and residents, garnered attention from the Public Improvements Committee, which authorized $300 for new tree planting. The village board also let a $75 contract to the American Park Company to trim trees and remove dead shrubbery along the river in 1914.[60]

In the late 1920s, at the behest of Riverside Garden Club members, residents were asked to help out the village in keeping the parkways clear. Riverside's village manager J. J. Obrien explained, "Vegetation has grown more rapidly this year than any time in ten years. . . . The tree branches hanging low force pedestrians to take a wetting or get off the sidewalk." He recommended trimming overhanging branches to clear a seven-foot height. Also in 1928, the garden club catalyzed what has become in Riverside a controversial issue: public signage. The club cited the intersection of Burlington and Longcommon Roads as dangerous for automobile traffic, and thus the village erected the first of many signs to come.[61] Signage is often seen as a man-made intrusion on the natural landscape, yet in today's litigious world, signs are often required.

Riverside's population increased more between 1920 and 1930 than in any other decade, from about 2,500 to 6,700. Toward the end of the 1920s, many new homes had been built, reflecting the post–World War I boom times. Many lots were subdivided, from the original 100-foot width to 50-foot. National trends since the early 1900s had paved the way for zoning laws in large cities such as New York, Los Angeles, and San Francisco. Chicago had formed a zoning commission in 1919, and the State of Illinois passed a zoning law in 1921 that provided municipalities with powers to enact local zoning laws. Riverside thus created its own zoning commission in 1921 and ordinance in May 1922 that established the "character, type, and intensity of use of every parcel of land in the Village."[62]

Olmsted had been well aware of the threats to the desirability of suburbs if there were no checks on the growth and use of residential properties. Developers of his era relied on nuisance laws and design guidelines. But nuisance laws were notoriously difficult to legally enforce, and design guidelines (such as the curving roads and parkway tree plantings in Riverside) were also subject to change. As author Robert M. Fogelson notes, "By the late nineteenth century, even Olmsted realized that the guidelines by themselves were not enough to bring about a high degree of permanence in suburbia."[63] Newer suburbs, such as Roland Park in Baltimore (designed by the Olmsted brothers), incorporated very restrictive covenants in their deeds in the 1890s. Restricted deeds became popularized such that, according to Fogelson, by the 1920s many "middle-class subdivisions were restricted."[64]

Riverside relied on zoning rather than on restrictive covenants tied to deeds. The proliferation of new apartment buildings in nearby Chicago neighborhoods created a major impetus to the village's new zoning law. But, as a *Chicago Tribune* headline declared, "Riverside Locks the Stable after the Horse Is Gone."[65] At issue were the Link Manor apartments built on Longcommon Road. The eighteen-unit complex, despite being designed by locally famous Prairie school architect E. E. Roberts, concerned residents who preferred single-family homes. In this aspect, the original Riverside design departs from contemporary master-planned communities that emphasize a diverse mix of housing alternatives. Yet, retaining the predominance of single-family homes seemed important for preserving the suburban character of Olmsted's design.

October 29, 1929, brought new construction to a standstill in Riverside and throughout America. During the Great Depression, many undeveloped lots in Riverside became eyesores. The village urged residents to clean up vacant lots and drag refuse to the parkway where village employees could haul it away.[66] No new apartments, no new houses: in spite of itself, Riverside preserved its architecture and landscape through the hard times.

The rise of sports in urban parks in the United States largely occurred in the late 1800s, the result of many factors including a decline in Puritanism, strong promotion, and even the popularity of the Kodak camera.[67] Golf was introduced to the Olmsted-designed Franklin Park in Boston around 1890, much to the later chagrin of John C. Olmsted, who claimed, "The introduction of golf-playing is an unwise sacrifice of the pleasure and comfort of many in the quiet enjoyment of the park."[68] It was the notion of the "fast-moving ball" that might disturb the contemplative spirit of those enjoying passive recreation in the green space that distressed the younger Olmsted. Although many cities claim title to oldest golf course in America, Riverside men first nurtured their love of golf on a three-hole course across from William A. Havemeyer's house on the Longcommon.[69] Soon, however, they recognized that a proper course required more land, and a group of twenty-two Riversiders formed the Riverside Golf Club. Among the founders was Havemeyer, relative and representative of the Havemeyers' sugar refining business, and also Theodore A. Havemeyer of New York, who founded the United States Golf Association in 1894.[70] In 1894, the Riverside Golf Club purchased eighty-five acres north of the village (in present-day North Riverside), sufficient for a nine-hole course. Sheep kept the greens trimmed. In 1914, the group bought an adjacent thirty acres and created an eighteen-hole course. The expanded course straddled the Des Plaines River, and the golf club planned to include boating and canoeing.[71]

The burgeoning popularity of golf throughout the United States expedited research into turf grasses by the U.S. Department of Agriculture.[72] As a byproduct of this research, grass species for the home grounds also improved. Chicago-area Vaughan's Nursery developed its own brand of grass seed and proudly displayed it at the World's Fair. Riverside lawns, and those of many Chicago area residences, became easier to maintain with the better seed.

Bicycling reached its heyday in Chicago in the 1890s. Wealthy individuals could afford earlier bicycles (such as "high wheelers" of the 1870s), but cheaper bicycles mass-produced at the end of the century appealed to the middle class. Chicago became known as the "bicycle-building capital of America," with about two-thirds of all bicycles made within 150 miles of the city.[73] Clubs of the so-called wheelmen sponsored rides throughout Chicago.

Riverside, which had its own club, became a popular destination because of its well-maintained streets. The Chicago Cycling Club headed for Riverside in July 1890, the Illinois Cycling Club in April 1892.[74] Two years later, Lucy Porter, a wheelwoman of some renown, startled spectators by wearing trousers while riding with the Illinois Cycling Club at Riverside. The *Chicago Tribune* reported, "The suit is extremely graceful and pretty with no hint of immodesty or unwomanliness. It consists of trousers exceedingly fully gathered at the knee; jersey leggins [sic] and a long coat-like basque with vest and revers [type of lapel]."[75]

With her jaunty bicycle cap, Porter nonetheless confided her initial nervousness at being the first Chicago woman to wear the attire. "I fully expected to be hooted and hissed and yelled at all along the route, but, though people stopped and stared at me, I was not the recipient of any insulting attention." Porter declared that the outfit enabled her to double her speed, even riding into the wind.[76]

In the bicycling season opener of April 1896, Riverside was declared the most popular journey for most of Chicago's many bicycle clubs. The *Chicago Tribune* reported, "Riverside seemed to be the favorite destination of the cyclists as the condition of the roads to that suburb is generally as good as can be found."[77]

In 1892 the National Lawn Tennis Association Western Amateur tournament was played at Riverside.[78] Teams from the Pacific Coast, Detroit, and other American regions mingled with Riversiders including the Havemeyers, Shermans, Mundys, Ameses, and others. Tennis courts were initially located along Quincy Avenue before the business district expanded.

A river club formed in fall of 1912, open to all Riversiders and nearby neighborhoods.[79] Activities included maintaining the Des Plaines in good condition for winter skating and canoeing to such destinations as Starved Rock and Libertyville.

NOTES FROM THE PROGRESSIVES

During the Progressive Era, the City Beautiful movement radiated throughout the United States and elsewhere as an outgrowth of the World's Columbian Exposition. Inspired by the fair's combination of architecture, landscape, art, and site planning, proponents of the movement hoped to revive cities and uplift their residents by making their surroundings more beautiful. In Chicago, this took the form of the 1909 *Plan of Chicago*, authored primarily by architect Daniel Burnham. Other cities, such as Washington, D.C., Kansas City, Louisville, and the Florida suburb of Coral Gables, expanded or revised their layout to emulate City Beautiful ideals.

Riverside already embodied most of the City Beautiful elements, although its naturalistic design did not adhere to the often formal, Beaux Arts motifs of the City Beautiful movement. Nonetheless, Riverside residents were not immune to the call to "beautify" the neighborhood, with the newly formed garden club offering its opinions of flower decoration. The gardenesque aspect of the new decorations likely would not have impressed Olmsted, who wrote of the simple beauty of an unadorned town with "no village improvement association, no branch of the Art Decorative, no reading club for the art periodicals, no park or parklet, no soldiers' monument, no fountains, no florist's establishment, not a single glass house, no bedding plants, no ribbon gardening, no vases, no lawn mowers, no rustic work, nothing from Japan, in all the long street."[80]

The issue of protecting public, taxpayer-funded amenities from outside users has plagued developers for decades. Olmsted and Vaux were quite cognizant of the potential growth of cities and their likely encroachment. The design and siting of Central Park, for example, took into account the likely expansion of Manhattan. Their design for Riverside included two potential insulating elements: belts of woods and shrubbery at the margins of the development, and a main entryway (never completed) of the proposed parkway leading to the village.

Today's suburban communities are often gated with electronic access. Additionally, residential vehicle stickers are used to distinguish among rightful and external users of streets and parking. In earlier developments, such as Llewellyn, a manned gatehouse prevented visitors. Riverside, with no physical barriers to entry on two sides, needed to resort to public use restrictions (for example, on fishing) that limited residents as well as outsiders.

Zoning emerged as the twentieth-century solution for Riverside to proscribe unwanted forms of building. Unlike some contemporary suburbs, restrictive covenants were not used particularly to exclude "undesirable" groups of people but rather behaviors. According to historian Fogelson, "People were undesirable because of what they did, because of how they used (or, more precisely, misused) the land—how, through 'ignorance, incompetence, bad taste or knavery,' they allowed rural buildings and fences to decay, cut down tall trees and polluted sparkling streams, defaced the countryside with shops, factories, stables, brickyards, beer gardens, and dram shops and otherwise destroyed the bucolic setting that had drawn them to suburbia in the first place."[81]

Nonetheless, during the Progressive Era, communities, while zoned differently, often shared resources and thus needed to work together. Riverside relied on both individual efforts and local consortiums to ensure that the shared resource, the Des Plaines River, remained clear. Riversiders took a lead role in marshaling resources to combat water pollution as upstream contaminants took their toll. This external force affected many nearby watershed communities, but the river, in Olmsted's day and for many years later, still commanded priorities and action in the bucolic namesake village.

Many of the major changes in Riverside during the Progressive Era were outgrowths of external movements or technologies. Social movements wherein inner-city working poor traveled by streetcar to the nearby suburbs likely fueled Riversiders' enthusiasm for the creation of the forest preserves as an alternative destination and early adoption of zoning laws against multifamily dwellings. Nowadays, city planning encourages a diversity of incomes, and vacant surrounding land is unlikely to be available to a new development. Today's increase in remote working may alter many suburbs' demographics, and those with preservation ideals should be attuned to the changes. Progressive Era conservation efforts along with the City Beautiful movement spilled into Riverside and made residents more appreciative of the natural habitats within the village limits. Although electrification and other technological improvements offered indoor alternatives, during the Progressive Era the outdoors espoused by Olmsted still beckoned Riverside residents.

Scout Cabin, built by Boy Scouts and Riverside men on the eve of the Depression, lies on the banks of the Des Plaines River. Dedicated in November 1928, its rustic design blends with the surrounding Indian Garden natural area. Photo by William Suriano.

CHAPTER 5

Depression through the Atomic Age (1930–1969)

If a stranger were blindfolded, whisked to the heart of Riverside, Illinois, and then permitted to look about, he would probably never suspect that he was standing in a prairie oasis, and that just beyond the confines of his vision lay gangster-ridden Cicero and all the endless gridiron and monotony of the western Chicago region. After he had seen the long curving Common with an elm-arched road on each side, and the attractive houses already of some age, facing the common and set well back from the road in the midst of trees and shrubs, the stranger would doubtless believe that he was in the midst of a New England village.[1]

So wrote landscape architect and city planner Howard Menhinick in his 1932 retrospective of Riverside in *Landscape Architecture Magazine*. Despite the curious mix of prairie and New England references in the essay by Michigan-born, Harvard-trained Menhinick, the magazine's accompanying photographs demonstrated that much of Olmsted's design remained sixty years later.

Riverside had endured financial panics and World War I, but the effects of the Great Depression and World War II would severely test the community. At the start of the Depression, much of Riverside's land had already been developed; only the northwest quadrant remained vacant. The undeveloped land, with its sandy soil still present from ancient beach ledges, became the de facto playground for children in the village. Roads there had been laid out according to Olmsted's plan but remained unpaved—little more than ruts in the prairie sod.

The Great Depression dwarfed the effects of previous financial crises, but, despite severe hardships, Riverside residents weathered the storm and protected their community. Most assuredly, there were losses—of homes, lives, and, due to Dutch elm disease, Riverside greenery. The federal government, in its relief programs such as the Works Progress Administration, directly shaped recreation and usage of Riverside's green space. The effects of the WPA, meant to be a short-term program, still reverberate in Riverside's green space usage today.

As post–World War II home construction boomed, questions of preservation arose. Mid-century modern designs with integrated household updates such as air conditioning, streamlined furnishings, and family "rec rooms" rendered obsolete older housing stock with their front porches, victory gardens, and parlors. In the 1950s, starkly different restoration efforts for two of Riverside's major homes, the Babson and Coonley estates, would push the preservation question to a clear test. But before any architectural restoration began, Riverside needed to examine the very health of its own village.

PUBLIC HEALTH AND BUGS: "EVERY MOSQUITO IS A POTENTIAL MURDERER"

As a leader in the U.S. Sanitary Commission in the Civil War, Olmsted created Riverside as a healthy alternative to the unsanitary

This aerial view of Riverside, ca. 1938, shows the incomplete northeast quadrant with roads laid out, but no homes (upper right in photo). The Coonley estate is at bottom left and the Babson estate top center. Author's collection.

conditions in crowded cities. A firm believer in the health benefits of outdoor exercise such as walking, Olmsted's emphasis on beauty and green space helped lure people to nature. Beginning in the Progressive Era and continuing through the 1930s and 1940s, Riverside codified several programs promoting good health. The Riverside School District mandated vaccinations as they became available. The village board created the Department of Public Health in 1922 to address the growing concern of communicable diseases such as scarlet fever, tuberculosis, and others. The board appointed Dr. Spencer S. Fuller as its health commissioner, a position he retained for many years.

Dr. Fuller offered this window into Riverside's public health in his 1934 annual assessment: "The whole report is an excellent record and I doubt if it can be equaled by any village this size in the state."[2] Of the 201 contagious diseases reported, the most prevalent was mumps followed by chicken pox, scarlet fever, and whooping cough. The incidence of these diseases was less than that in crowded cities, but Riverside faced its own unique battle with a fear of malaria and other mosquito-borne illnesses.

Mosquitoes created an ongoing nuisance and health risk. When Olmsted reviewed the site in his *Preliminary Report*, neighbors had dismissed the problem. "We nowhere found, even among the bushes near the water, on a warm August evening, any mosquitoes or lake flies, though both were at the time annoying the people of Chicago," Olmsted assured the investors.[3] Science had definitively proven the link between mosquitoes and malaria by 1900, replacing the miasma theory with the germ theory. Coincident with a mosquito-related tragedy in Riverside, the *Chicago Tribune* declared an all-out war against the insects in 1914. The tragedy had involved a two-year-old Riverside girl who died from burns after pouring carbolic acid on herself. Carbolic acid, used sparingly, had been the remedy of choice for mosquito bites.[4]

The Riverside Women's Club sounded an early anti-mosquito rallying cry, blaming the Des Plaines River for the source of the insects. Although the *Tribune*'s medical columnist, W. A. Evans, MD, initially opined that Riverside's mosquito issue resulted from open home cisterns, not the Des Plaines River, a few months later he would concede that the damming of the river had caused mosquito breeding grounds.[5]

Early mosquito battles, fought with sprays of kerosene and crude oil, required children to stay indoors after dusk. Finally, in 1924, Riverside businessman George A. Hughes and other residents spearheaded legislation in Springfield to create a mosquito abatement district.[6] Hughes would become the first chairman of the Des Plaines Valley Sanitary Association, whose purpose was mosquito eradication.[7] "Every mosquito is a potential murderer," Hughes claimed. Spencer Fuller agreed: "A mother mosquito brings forth a litter every five days."[8] An early proponent of separating sewers and stormwater in municipal systems, Fuller lobbied for a sewer intercept in the Des Plaines as early as 1930, to improve water quality and help keep the channel clear of debris.[9] Part of the problem lay in George Hofmann's refusal to open the dam (since his land was affected), behind which sewage collected. Instead of engaging in lengthy court battles with Hofmann, Riverside's village board elected to dig a channel around the dam so that the water could flow through and clear contaminants that presumably drew mosquitoes. This channeling was performed under police guard lest objections rise to a violent level.[10]

"Skeeter Plague Called Worst in City's History," trumpeted a *Chicago Tribune* headline in May 1933.[11] By then, Fuller had assumed the chair of the Des Plaines Valley Mosquito Abatement District, and on his recommendations, spraying would commence.[12] The district started using a concoction of soap, kerosene, and insecticide powder to eradicate the pests. These efforts well

preceded the National Malaria Eradication Program of 1947, which also involved spraying and draining.

Mosquito abatement and protections of nature sometimes collided. An effort by the Chicago Sanitary District to deepen the channel of the river met resistance. According to the *Chicago Tribune*, Hughes and Fuller, along with residents of Riverside's Maplewood section, objected to the proposed channeling "for fear that trees along the river would be destroyed by a temporary lowering of the water level and spoil the natural beauty of the river."[13]

The abatement program succeeded, so much so that other municipalities joined. In 1939, under Dr. Fuller's presidency on the Mosquito Abatement District, nearby townships banded together to ensure that their geographical area would be included in spraying.[14] By 1941 Dr. Fuller lead the tri-county mosquito program, which included fifty-seven townships. The four-year, $4 million program, with the help of the WPA, sought to identify and drain areas deemed "wastelands" around Chicago in the interest of eradicating mosquitoes.[15]

Widespread use of DDT, used in World War II, began in the Chicago area in 1946, just one year after first being offered for public sale. The Des Plaines Valley Mosquito Abatement District had experimented with the chemical a year before. Lyell Clarke, Riversider and a chief engineer with the district, announced it would be used in garbage dumps and catch basins but not in streams, as it was fatal to fish.[16] Fears of a link between mosquitoes and polio, along with a spike in that disease, caused neighboring Lyons to request that its whole village be sprayed.

Two years later, the Des Plaines Valley Mosquito Abatement District sprayed its entire jurisdictional area with DDT fogging machines. The *Tribune* quoted Clarke as promising that the spray would not harm humans or animals.[17] In 1949, the Illinois Natural Survey concluded that DDT would not harm birds and therefore

This American elm in Guthrie Park is one of the few that has survived Dutch elm disease. Photo by author.

could be used in the Cook County Forest Preserves. Part of its conclusion was based on experimental tests such as that on the Des Plaines River in Riverside, where the water was "misted" three times with a DDT blower.[18]

Still, early objections to DDT arose, and mounting evidence about the chemical's dangers ultimately changed the district's usage. The Izaak Walton League protested the use of sprays as being dangerous to wildlife. Renowned author Rachel Carson published her seminal book on the dangers of pesticides, *Silent Spring*, in 1962. By 1965, the Des Plaines Valley Mosquito Abatement District adopted a multiprong attack against the bug. Although DDT still headlined the arsenal, now the district populated streams and ponds with mosquito fish (*Gambusia affinis*), thought to eradicate the larvae.[19] By 1969, the City of Chicago Park District discontinued use of DDT, and Riverside looked to other weapons to fight the mosquito war.

Mosquitoes were not the only pests that threatened Riverside's character. Bark beetles, burrowing under protective tree layers, spread the deadly fungi responsible for Dutch elm disease. First noted in the United States in the late 1920s, Dutch elm disease had by the 1950s spread to the southern two-thirds of Illinois. Dr. Richard Campana, Dutch elm disease expert and Illinois Natural Survey plant pathologist, warned in 1958, "The problem of Dutch Elm disease is a grim economic reality which no municipality with many elms can afford to disregard."[20]

With an estimated 10,000 elm trees in Riverside's public and private land, village officials took the threat seriously.[21] In a seminal stewardship act, the village board created a Forestry Advisory Committee in 1957. The committee would consult as to the types of trees to plant and the maintenance needed to thwart such dangers as Dutch elm disease. Spraying trees with a DDT emulsion was the popular weapon of choice. The effect of pesticides such as DDT on humans awaited confirmation.

Community efforts also aimed to reduce the Dutch elm threat. The Riverside Garden Club hosted a flower show at the old Ripley mansion on Michaux Road to raise funds for Dutch elm disease eradication. Residents were asked to be on the lookout for signs of the disease. In 1965, a new ordinance specified rules on when and why affected trees could be removed. By 1969, about forty trees per year succumbed to the disease, and the village began replacing the trees with oaks and maples. This began a conscious effort to create plant diversity with an eye toward disease prevention.

PARKS AND RECREATION WITH THE WPA: "BOONDOGGLING, IF YOU INSIST"

Olmsted's vision of the promenade, especially in the unrealized boulevard linking Riverside to Chicago, epitomized, for him, community socialization. Each era brought new ideas of how to use green space. Beginning in the early 1900s, the playground movement took hold in Chicago, spearheaded by Progressive reformers such as Jane Addams and implemented by landscape architects such as Jens Jensen and the Olmsted brothers, which emphasized outdoor play for children. Questions had already arisen in Riverside about entertainments for youth. Supervised play, especially during the summer when children enjoyed substantial leisure time, seemed the antidote to idle hands. Yet, funding issues and debates over use of public land delayed formal recreation programs in the village.

The drumbeat for supervised recreation, particularly for children, intensified across the nation with the public works projects of the Depression. The federal Works Progress Administration (later renamed the Work Projects Administration) and its predecessor, the Civil Works Administration, emphasized enhanced community recreation programs and facilities. A WPA report noted not only that recreation projects supplied work to the unemployed but also that "progress has also been made towards another program objective—the incorporation of recreational services as a permanent local function."[22] Pundits espoused the need for group recreation—extending from bridge games to arts and crafts to outdoor sports—to fill the increased leisure time now experienced by adults and youth due to labor-saving devices or unemployment.

Riversiders vacillated on the need for supervised recreation. Some efforts had been made, especially in summer, to offer programs through the public schools. Fears about the nefarious effects of movie theaters on young minds begged for a "wholesome" solution. In 1934, Riverside's public school PTA invited Henry Forman, author of *Our Movie Made Children*, to lecture on the evils of the talking pictures. The movies of 1934 (such as *It Happened One Night* and *The Gay Divorcée*), with their "vivid and glamorous presentation," represented an education system "wholly haphazard, unsupervised, and dangerous."[23] Something needed to be done!

The WPA provided physical, social, cultural, and therapeutic recreation programs, often constructing facilities to house the activities. Nationwide, 60 percent of the participants were under age sixteen, 26 percent were between ages sixteen and twenty-five, and the balance were over twenty-five.[24] Many of the WPA and Civil Works Administration projects were intended for urban areas, which lacked green space, or for rural areas, which lacked access to city entertainment. Riverside, which lacked neither, nonetheless jumped on the bandwagon to increase supervised recreation.

The experiment was not without controversy. Villagers proposed that playgrounds near Ames school, Robinson Court, Swan Pond, and Indian Garden should include flower gardens to be designed and maintained by various women's clubs. An athletic field for Indian Garden (then defined as stretching from the Kroehler/Coonley estate to Hofmann Dam) was hotly disputed by residents

WPA work included stone staircases at Swan Pond. Photo by author.

of the First Division. Proponents (180 of whom signed a petition started by local resident O. H. Fairchild, who organized sports for children) noted that recent channel blasting by the Sanitary District had left piles of rockwork on the riverbank and that the unsightly area could be transformed into a needed play space.[25] Detractors argued that the athletic fields would cause increased traffic with attendant safety issues and would threaten the peace of nearby residents.

The ambitious plan, dependent on Civil Works Administration funding, included a football field, three tennis courts, several baseball diamonds, a play space for young children, a riverbank drive to be built on a raised dike, and parking for 300 cars. The athletic fields would be screened from Fairbank Road with appropriate shrubbery and trees. The proposed project pitted neighbor against neighbor, with a newspaper editorial scolding, "The history of Riverside as well as the history of other communities is filled with instances where certain sections have been 'discriminated against' in favor of the whole community."[26] Although this entire plan was not realized, many pieces of it—particularly the changes to the riverbank—were put into operation.

National focus on the need for public recreation resulted in multiple studies at the state and local levels. In one exhaustive multivolume report by the Chicago Planning Commission and Northwestern University, several metrics described the latest thinking on the appropriate amount of parkland per person. George Kingery, director of the Chicago Regional Planning Association, advised 10 acres of park (including 3 acres of playgrounds) per 1,000 residents. Other experts recommended 1 acre of park/playground per 125 residents. This study, conducted between 1934 and 1936, compared all suburbs and calculated Riverside at 123.7 acres of park/playground per 7,140 residents (17.3 acres per 1,000 persons), easily surpassing the recommended amount.[27]

The *Riverside News* reported in 1935 that "a supervised recreation project for Riverside (or boondoggling[,] if you insist) appeared to be very much 'in the bag' this week" after a visit from a WPA representative. The WPA rep, whose job was to secure community sponsorship, met with the PTA chair, local health authority, and others to convince them of the need for supervised recreation.[28]

The Chicago Regional Planning Association also conducted a survey of recreation needs and availability in the Chicago region. Its report found that Riverside, despite an embarrassment of riches in green space, lacked recreation opportunities. "Standing high in public park land among Chicago's suburbs Riverside still does not have the recreation and playground facilities recommended for the communities of today," reported the *Riverside News* in a synopsis of the 1937 regional planning report.[29] Although the amount of parkland was generous and suitably distributed throughout the village, the regional report sought more playground equipment and supervised, organized programs as desired in urban areas. The report was largely concerned with organized play and permanent structures rather than passive recreation (walking, nature viewing, and the like). Thus began the introduction of playground equipment into the Olmsted greenswards.

By 1937, WPA funding for such programs was contingent on municipalities creating or already having a recreation organization in place. Faced with losing WPA funding, Riverside put the question of creating a local recreation board to a referendum in April 1937. This proposed board, at an average cost to taxpayers of $1.25 per annum, would secure the WPA funds.[30] Concerned about the viability of WPA funding, village president Harry Taylor forecast, "We should be prepared to take over the recreation project and not let it collapse because of lack of an organization to handle it." The local recreation board, established by ordinance in June 1937, then authorized the construction of tennis courts and shuffleboards in later ordinances in the fall of that year.

As different suburbs and Chicago areas invested in recreation facilities such as swimming pools and fieldhouses, with associated programs, their taxpayers started to understand the popularity problems Riverside had faced for decades. The Chicago Recreation Commission reported about other communities, "Local municipal recreation authorities mention many examples of irresponsibility on the part of outsiders . . . and a good deal of local feeling against the intrusion of visitors."[31] Irresponsible alcohol use reigned as the chief complaint, along with vandalism and health issues in swimming pool hygiene. Riverside was cited as an example in this discussion: "Riverside, which has always taken pride in its park setting, has not counted the neighboring Brookfield Zoo and forest preserve an unmixed blessing." Quoting Dr. Fuller, the report stated, "These . . . benefits are also disrupting forces, for they bring into the community or along its borders millions of visitors every year. The future of Riverside will depend to great extent upon what control is placed upon these outside influences."[32]

When the Brookfield Zoo officially opened (on land west of the river in Olmsted's plan) in July 1934, more than 58,000 visitors arrived. Prior to opening, zoo officials gave a preview of the zoo to the press and representatives from local governments. Zoo director Edward H. Bean predicted the zoo would be the greatest trade stimulant ever enjoyed by nearby towns and that 2 million people would visit each year. Herbert Bassman, then president of Riverside's chamber of commerce, presided over the preview and presentations. "The zoological gardens will not be a detriment to nearby or distant municipalities," Bean promised.[33]

A *Chicago Tribune* map to the zoo featured two main routes through Riverside. Autoists could drive down Longcommon Road, or train excursionists could debark at the Riverside station and walk the mile or so to the zoo.[34] Other routes included the street-cars or major roads that bordered Riverside. In the first few years, traffic police were needed to control visitors on Forest Avenue and also Thirty-First Street in Riverside. When First Avenue was extended to Ogden Avenue, however, the *Riverside News* noted a decrease in Riverside traffic.[35]

Overall, the zoo and neighboring forest preserves did not cause many Riverside complaints and surely were an improvement over the threat in the early part of the century of beer gardens and amusement parks. Perhaps some of the credit can be given Charles Sauers, who managed the forest preserves with great energy and political savvy. "Captain" Sauers, the general superintendent of the Cook County Forest Preserves from 1929 to 1964, lived on Olmsted Road in Riverside. He was a man both practical and creative, and under his leadership, the forest preserves were to be kept as naturalistic as possible. Recognizing his affinity for natural design, the Chicago Society of Landscape Architects voted him as their president in 1935.[36] He spearheaded construction of picnic shelters and trails for visitors' safety and nature enjoyment, as well as to protect the preserves. Riverside, and other nearby communities, also benefited from designated picnic areas, which reduced the number of interlopers seeking a picnic spot in the surrounding villages.

The Des Plaines River continued to offer recreational activities to forest preserve visitors. Yet, because of the pollution, "from Irving Park Road to southward to Riverside you can kiss the river good-bye as a pleasure stream," said Roberts Mann, conservation expert with the forest preserves after an exploratory survey of the river.[37] Mann and Sauers agreed that the ultimate, but expensive, solution required a separation of sewer water and stormwater to compensate for the increased development upstream of Riverside.

In the early 1950s, Cook County created the citizen-led "clean streams committee," which surveyed river and stream conditions and reported pollution sources to the government. Duke Reed, of Riverside, was appointed to lead the Salt Creek team. The persistent pollution of the Des Plaines River and associated tributaries like Salt Creek created the impetus for forming the committee. Reed, who continued this volunteer work for years, expanded his territory to the whole Des Plaines watershed and reported on many point-source pollution culprits. Reed described dumping of toxic waste and even heavy materials such as tombstones, describing one oil slick from Cermak Road to Riverside as the worst since World War II.[38] By 1963, Reed had assumed the chairmanship of the overall clean streams committee, Henry Miller of Riverside volunteered to lead the lower Des Plaines portion, and another Riversider, Franklin Wray, had been assigned to the Des Plaines Valley Mosquito Abatement District.[39] Riverside's early conservationists kept the pressure on elected officials to maintain sanitary conditions throughout the river valley. Pollution would be a continuing problem for Riverside and its neighboring towns, requiring constant stewardship.

HOMES AND GARDENS: "HOMES OF TOMORROW"

Smaller homes and streamlined modern styles became the national rage in the 1930s through the 1950s. Larger Victorian homes gave way to bungalows to satisfy increases in population but shrinking budgets. Riverside more than doubled its population in the ten boom years from 1920 (2,532) to 1930 (6,770), and it is no wonder that, despite the Depression, local forecasts called for increased population. One 1937 estimate predicted Riverside's population at more than 15,000 by 1960.[40] The estimate seemed reasonable at the time, since less than half of the platted lots had been built: there were 1,820 residences and 2,616 vacant lots in Riverside.[41] (Had the city planners a crystal ball, however, they would have seen Riverside's population top out at 10,357 in 1970 and decline to about 8,800 from there.)

The hobbled economy caused many historic homes to be lost. Several homes featured in the Riverside Improvement Company's 1871 promotional booklet were razed: the Murray/Havemeyer residence at 176 Nuttall (built by William Le Baron Jenney with landscape diagram by Olmsted firm) (1937); the 1871 Chase home (1934); artist H. C. Ford's home (1940). Realtor Henry Miller advised the downstate owner of the Havemeyer home, which had been subjected to teenage vandalism, that leveling the house would be best. Similarly, Miller worked with the bank that owned the Chase home, at Akenside and Michaux, to raze it to make way for smaller properties.

New homeowners in Riverside's northwest section built smaller homes, such as a Sears kit home. Other homeowners drew inspiration from the Century of Progress Exposition. This 1933–34 world's fair on Chicago's lakefront included a "Homes of Tomorrow" exhibit featuring full-size examples of houses that embraced the new technologies and tastes of the era. One home from the fair, a cube-like house on Southcote Road, was actually relocated to Riverside. A new home constructed on Selbourne Road featured an 18 x 11 roof garden over the attached garage.[42] Two new steel-framed homes, one on Longcommon and one on Delaplaine, drew headlines for the perceived structural integrity but also for the cost.

These smaller-footprint homes—whether a Sears kit or a smaller bungalow—fit neatly on the smaller subdivided lots. Unique to Riverside properties, however, was the shape of the backyard. Because of the curved streets, smaller backyards often meant areas that narrowed to pie-shaped wedges. With much of the backyard consumed by driveways leading to detached garages, little space was left to create elaborate gardens or the newfound private backyard retreats featured in many lifestyle magazines.

While most gardens in the Depression and World War II eras tended to the utilitarian, and vegetable or fruit crops predominated, other design tastes were explored. In 1935, the Riverside Garden Club hosted a speaker on English gardens.[43] Shady gardens became of interest as Riverside's trees matured into overhead canopies. Another association, the Garden Lovers Club of Riverside, began an intensive study into native plants.[44] Riverside sponsored a talk in the Township Hall by pioneering landscape architect Annette Hoyt Flanders in 1943, "Small Gardens for Houses, Old and New," with more than 400 attendees expected from the West Suburban Garden Clubs group.[45]

The Riverside Garden Club planted lilacs throughout the village—more than 100, including several French varieties.[46] Lilacs became fashionable in the 1930s, with the *Chicago Tribune* cosponsoring with the Chicago Plant, Flower and Fruit Guild the distribution of lilac bouquets to hospitalized and other individuals. Riversiders participated in "Lilac Day" from 1929 through 1942, donating baskets of lilacs for the poor and ill and sending via the CB&Q to Union Station. When wartime activities precluded use of rail and truck transportation for that purpose, members of the plant guild continued the tradition on their own.

Somewhere between the Great Depression and the Atomic Age, Riverside homeowners acquired the aesthetic for evergreen foundation plants. Likely following the national trend of streamlined modernity for home and garden, rows of clipped yews replaced mixed woody shrubs at the base of many houses. This popular but overused garden feature persists today, although some Riverside homes feature interesting mixes of evergreen and deciduous shrubs.

Foundation plantings had been in fashion in the 1920s and even earlier. A host of books and articles on the subject were published in the late 1920s, including Frank Waugh's essay "Foundation Planting" and Leonard Johnson's book *Foundation Planting*.

Authors Cynthia Girling and Kenneth Helphand argue that American foundation plantings are a way of bringing the European hedge closer from the street to the house. The American lawn thus becomes the interface between public property and private.[47] In the 1950s, the types of foundation plantings shifted from deciduous to evergreen because the latter could be sheared in a straight line to complement the linear architecture of the home.

A TALE OF TWO HOUSES: "WE'RE TRYING TO MAKE A LIVING"

Without doubt, two homes figure as Riverside's most elaborate properties: the Avery Coonley home and the Babson estate. Construction on the Coonley property, comprising four separate structures designed by Frank Lloyd Wright and two by his apprentice John Drummond, began around 1907 and finished in 1913.

The Babson estate, designed by Louis Sullivan with grounds designed by Jens Jensen, was razed. Village of Riverside, Riverside Historical Commission.

The estate included the main house, a separate Gardener's Cottage, stables, a school/playhouse for the owners' daughter, and, later, a teachers' home and caretaker's cottage (the latter two designed Drummond). Wright himself called the estate one of his most successful projects. Jens Jensen designed the grounds in a naturalistic style, emphasizing his signature plants: hawthorns, crabapples, and prairie roses.

At about the same time, Henry Babson and his wife hired Louis Sullivan to build an estate on twenty-eight acres, on lots including those once owned by Olmsted, facing the ballpark on the Longcommon. Babson first moved to Chicago to work at the World's Columbian Exposition. Immersed in the new technologies of recording machines, he made his fortune distributing Victor phonographs and investing in other innovative technologies. The Babson mansion featured twenty-five rooms with exquisite Sullivan-designed windows overlooking a landscape designed by Jens Jensen.

The Babsons offered the home to the village in 1945, stipulating only that it should be named in honor of their deceased son and that it be used for a public park and recreation center. The village sought the expert advice of Lebert H. Weir of the National Recreation Association. More than 1,200 Riverside residents approved of the donation, but a vocal bloc of dissenters argued that Riverside possessed enough park space, that the building maintenance costs would mushroom, and that taxes would continually rise. Furthermore, according to the *Chicago Tribune*, the bloc noted that the Babson gift was conditioned on the space being enjoyed by Riverside residents *and* the public at large. Thus, "any citizen of Cook County might have use of the property as much as the people of Riverside, which would result in the creation of a forest preserve with picnic grove in the heart of Riverside."[48] The thirty or so people opposing the bequest included Arnold Skow, who later developed the Coonley estate.

In 1956, developer William Baltis bought the property for $300,000. In a $3.5 million subdivision called "Virginia Heritage Estates," he initially planned to build Colonial-style homes, replete with modern TV rooms and, in a nod to the times, basement bomb shelters.[49] The forty homes would cost between $65,000 and $125,000. Ultimately, the design of the homes, built throughout the 1960s, reflected mid-century modern styles, such as split-level ranches.

The razing of the Babson estate raised the ire of preservationists—prescient individuals who were few in number. Jim Paul, who helped Baltis sell the homes, recalls, "When we started the development the newspapers were writing about Baltis built homes and about Mr. Paul [himself] tearing down the estate. There was a preservationist by the name of Richard Nickel who was writing letters to me and to the papers urging us to save the Babson house, endow it, and make it into a museum. Nickel was a young man; he couldn't have been more than twenty-eight or twenty-nine years old. I said, 'We're businessmen. We're trying to make a living for our families.'"[50]

Today, we may wince at the lost treasure, but it is hard to find fault with the individuals directly involved. As Paul recounts, "We didn't realize the importance of things like the hardware designed by Louis Sullivan. . . . Every Saturday and Sunday the front lawn was covered with cars and they [the hired house wrecker] were selling pieces of oak flooring, pieces of trim, doorknobs, etc. I never realized how important those pieces were. Some of the salvaged pieces from that house are in the Metropolitan Museum of Art in New York."[51] The Riverside Historical Museum now houses the dining room chandelier and wall sconces from the Babson estate.

The story of the Coonley estate followed a much different trajectory. Avery and Queene Ferry Coonley chose several vacant lots between Bloomingbank and Scottswood Roads, as well as nearby lots, to build their extensive Prairie-style estate designed by Frank Lloyd Wright in 1907. When the Coonleys relocated to Washington,

D.C., furniture magnate Peter Kroehler bought the estate in the 1920s. Wright visited the properties in 1937 and approved of Kroehler's modifications.[52] By the 1950s, however, much of the estate, which included freestanding homes, had been sold, and the main building of about 9,000 square feet languished.

Local architect Arnold Skow became interested in razing the building and subdividing the property for new ranch-style homes. Wright, then enjoying a renaissance in his career, intervened and dissuaded Peter Kroehler's widow from dismantling the estate in 1951.[53] As when Olmsted deterred Emery Childs from building on the Longcommon, Wright's words resonated. Art Institute professors Carolyn and Jim Howlett, who had bought and converted the estate's stables into a single-family home, raised awareness of the property's historic value by successfully pitching the story to national magazines, which took up the cause. Thus, with national exposure and the artist's own words, the Coonley estate was saved. The challenge, as in the Babson estate, would be to save historic structures and landscapes when their creator was gone.

Today, the Coonley main house and its separate structures are owned by seven different families. They have all been beautifully restored and also achieved individual National Historic Landmark status in 1970. Surely, the entreaties by Wright and the publicity attained through the Howletts' efforts affected the preservation of the estate—benefits the Babson estate did not have. It is a cautionary tale, however, for undiscovered works of art that may lack preservation today.

HISTORIC PRESERVATION EARLY STEPS: "DEPRESSION WAS THE REASON THE VOTE WAS NO"

Riverside's first major celebration of its own heritage in 1936 unfolded from a series of precipitating events. Chicago's leaders and

The main wing (shown here) of the Coonley estate has been restored, as have the other structures on the grounds. Photo by author.

boosters had created the Century of Progress World's Fair, not only to mark the city's centennial but also to jumpstart economic recovery and consumer confidence. Perhaps Riverside leaders derived inspiration from this very successful fair and its pretext for the fanfare. The village chose to celebrate its own centennial—but of a historical date of dubious importance. Descendants of the Forbes family, early settlers of the area now known as Riverside, declared 1936 as the centennial of their family's arrival.

Technological changes had also advanced despite the Depression and threatened to compromise Riverside's pastoral ambience. Refrigeration was becoming commonplace and, after the need for victory gardens waned, became a handy appliance for storing food and reducing trips to the grocery store. At the same time, more people had automobiles, and Riverside needed to consider the speed limits on its curving roads as horsepower and speed increased. The onset of air conditioning and the introduction of television presaged the coming decades when more Americans, including Riversiders, would spend time indoors.

Writing in the 1980s, Kenneth Jackson noted the turn of suburbanites from outdoor to indoor entertainment. Calling residential neighborhoods a "mass of small, private islands," Jackson noted how the decline of the front porch coupled with the popularity of the interior "family room" threatened the sense of community in suburbs. "The cult of domestic privatism, the desire to escape from the warm crowds of city streets, and the turning inward on the family have fully evolved since their articulation by Downing, Beecher, and Vaux a century and more earlier."[54]

The 1936 centennial raised awareness of Riverside's unique historic legacy and prompted several early preservation efforts. A book, *Riverside Then and Now*, was published chronicling the major milestones from presettlement to 1936. A historical society, first meeting in Catharine Mitchell's home, was formed and

Electrified refrigeration became more commonplace with a Riverside business, and homeowners had less need to grow fresh produce.
Village of Riverside, Riverside Historical Commission.

included Dr. Spencer Fuller, realtor wife Mrs. Henry A. Miller, and early settler descendant Miss Bessie Sherman, all of whom were later nominated as officers. The society, which would have sixty charter members within a few months, began with lectures of important nearby sites. "There are many historic sites in and near the community and one of our objectives should be to have these sites properly located and marked," said one of the society leaders in early 1937.[55] With lectures about Illinois history and the history of the Chicago Portage, the formative years of the Riverside Historical Society seemed to focus on everything but Riverside

THE WRECK IS HERE

BUT —

HE'S GONE

1938 SLOGAN
NO ACCIDENT DEATHS IN RIVERSIDE

The Cause?
Too Fast For Conditions
The Result?
One Dead and A Heap of Junk
The Answer?
Drive Carefully

A crashed car displayed in the 1930s cautioned Riverside drivers of the pitfalls of speeding on the curving roads. Author's collection.

itself. It was as if the founders recognized Riverside's geographic importance but not necessarily the historic importance of Olmsted's design.

This changed as the community matured in the next few decades. Undoubtedly, the controversies over the Babson and Coonley estates raised the profile of Riverside's own architectural heritage. But it was the relentless tug-of-war over the use of public landscapes that birthed Riverside's nonprofit preservation group, the Frederick Law Olmsted Society, in 1968. Even as the village recognized its upcoming centennial of the General Plan in 1969, some residents requested changes to the Longcommon to include a children's play area and ballpark. Robert Heidrich, then president of the Olmsted Society and also property owner across from the Longcommon, sued the village and acted as his own attorney, alleging that the new equipment violated the open space concept of Olmsted's design.[56]

These potential changes to the Longcommon prompted the Olmsted Society, with other villagers, to apply for National Landmark certification. The village received Illinois state certification as a landmark in 1969.[57] The National Historic Preservation Act, passed in 1966, just three years old when Riverside submitted its application, awarded the village a Historic Landscape Architecture District designation in 1970. The application emphasized Olmsted's design first, followed by architectural luminaries. Individual buildings were landmarked, but the entire village received landmark status due to Olmsted's design.

NOTES FROM THE DEPRESSION

The decades between 1930 and 1970 created perhaps the most extreme challenges for Riverside's signature design. The economy played a huge role. As one memoirist wrote, "The Depression was just there. I couldn't remember anything else. It caused some neighbors to move away. . . . I think the Depression was the reason the vote was 'No' to accepting a wonderful gift to the village from Mr. Babson of his estate grounds and Louis Sullivan's masterpiece mansion."[58]

The trade-off between active and passive recreation was not a new issue in city planning. Olmsted and Vaux had devised a solution with their segregated walkways and circulation routes in New York City's Central Park. But unadorned nature always seemed to beg for man-made ornamentation or new fads in sporting venues. Writing to Olmsted, fellow landscape architect H. W. S. Cleveland complained, "I get heart-sick and disgusted at times with the twaddle that passes for 'love of nature'—in the face of the evidence we have everywhere that to the great mass of the so called cultivated people nature has no attraction except when aided by the merest clap traps of fashionable entertainment which the real lover of nature seeks to escape from."[59] National programs, such as the WPA, are often one-size-fits-all, and the lure of promised funding must be weighed against the pragmatism of suitability for a unique community. In the WPA example, money was targeted to improve green space and programming in bereft communities. Riverside, awash in green space, nonetheless could not refuse the funding and succumbed to the siren call of supervised, structured outdoor programs and their attendant changes to the green design.

Suburban housing patterns influenced by Riverside, and yet widely different, were evident in the 1930s Federal Greenbelt Towns program and the post–World War II era Levittowns. The Greenbelt towns (in Greenbelt, Maryland; Greenhills, Ohio; and Greendale, Wisconsin) represented a New Deal effort to provide affordable housing in a new master-planned community. Like Riverside, all towns included walking paths and curves in their street design, modeled after the British Garden City movement

Turtle Park, a tot lot on the Longcommon, created a furor over proper use of green space. Photo by author.

of the early 1900s. A belt of green space, mostly intended for gardens, was planned for all towns. Yet, there, similarities ended. Greenhills and Greenbelt included many townhomes. Greenhills had virtually no front yards but is the only Greenbelt town with its encircling greenbelt intact. All the villages were federally owned until about the 1950s, with eligibility requirements to purchase a home.

Kenneth Jackson notes, "If imitation is the sincerest form of flattery, then William Levitt has been much honored in the past forty years."[60] Levitt & Sons' eponymous towns, erected near New York City, Philadelphia, and New Jersey, were mass-produced, budget-minded homes built to support the huge housing demand after the war. The town plans included curving streets and parks, but there, similarities to Riverside end. Built on bare farm fields, the Levitts bulldozed all existing trees. Standardized house designs predominated to maintain construction costs. Throughout the nation, builders in other cities copied the Levittown model, with the resultant growth of "cookie-cutter" subdivisions.

Historic homes were particularly threatened by the building booms of smaller homes following the Depression and World War II. In this case, national historic preservation movements, particularly the Historic Preservation Act, marked a major step in saving Olmsted's design. With the two examples of the Babson and Coonley estates, it was clear that decisions had to be made. Similarly, the continuous external threats posed to the Des Plaines River prompted Riverside residents to take leadership roles in mosquito abatement and continued battles against water pollution.

Curvilinear roads, popular in suburbs today, were a novel design element that Olmsted used to suggest leisure and pique interest in scenic vignettes. Photo by author.

CHAPTER 6

Historic Landmark to the
New Millennium (1971–2000)

The late twentieth century ushered in national laws and events that reverberated loudly in Riverside. The U.S. bicentennial in 1976 stoked preservation fever in cities and towns across America and prompted regional celebrations of history. Sweeping changes in national environmental laws inspired local responses. Demographic shifts altered the social patterns in communities.

Meanwhile, Olmsted scholarship and recognition of his work intensified, beginning with the Frederick Law Olmsted Papers Project of 1972, which, over the decades, published curated selections of the designer's seminal correspondence and works. The National Association for Olmsted Parks (now the Olmsted Network), founded in 1980, convened for its second annual conference in Chicago, with visits to Riverside. Meanwhile, the Chicago Friends of the Parks, Illinois Landmarks, and other advocacy groups fought a protracted battle to protect local landmarks, including Olmsted-designed parks.

Riverside's population had peaked in 1970, and, as new generations moved in, family sizes tended to be smaller. Large Victorian homes that could house five children and sundry servants no longer suited the lifestyles of new home buyers. Even as Victorian homes declined in popularity, Riverside lots became valuable as potential teardowns for mammoth McMansions with updated finishes and features. Preservation goals, hard-won through the village's landmark status, now needed enforceable ordinances to be effective.

FROM FORESTS TO LANDSCAPES: "LOSS HAS WEAKENED THE LANDSCAPE'S STRENGTH"

The nascent preservation movement in Riverside aimed to prevent misuse of the village's assets by ill-advised human intervention but had not contemplated natural disasters. The "tot lot" controversy on the Longcommon of the late 1960s foiled rampant building in the parks and led to an increased appreciation of Riverside's open spaces, trees, and landscape design. Reinforcing this sentiment, the village board upgraded the role of the Forest Advisory Commission (formerly the Forestry Advisory Committee) in 1973 to include tree selection and counsel on plant disease prevention. The commission included residents, especially those with some experience in the arborist field, with the hope of bringing more technical expertise.

In 1970 and 1971, with the advice of the Forest Advisory Commission, the village planted a total of 100 trees, many to replace those stricken by Dutch elm disease. Instead of elms, the commission recommended maples or Marshall ash, a green ash cultivar widely planted for its adaptability and vigor. Since 1965, this brought the grand total of new trees planted to nearly 450, or about 90 per year.[1]

The Forest Advisory Commission studied many alternatives to DDT and other chemicals to stave off the ravaging Dutch elm beetle. Although no magic bullet was found, Riverside's efforts did not go unnoticed. In fact, the EPA published a report that recommended a Riverside-based company, DeWill Inc., for its chemical alternative products, Elm Bark Beetle Trap and Beetle Lure.[2] To encourage more tree planting, the village instituted a "50-50" tree replacement program in 1979, whereby the village and homeowner would split the cost of a replacement tree on a parkway.[3]

Dutch elm disease brought the value of Riverside's trees into focus for many residents and the village trustees. By ordinance, residents were required to remove infected trees. As the signature archway of elm trees over Longcommon Road disappeared, residents appreciated their treasure of trees even more. After a village-sponsored tree inoculation program faltered, residents took matters into their own hands. A loosely banded group called the Neighborhood Elm Savers offered the fungicide Lignasan to residents for do-it-yourself treatment of trees on private property.[4]

In 1981, the Forest Advisory Commission was given authority to approve parkway plantings and recommend selections for public parks.[5] Professional consultants were tapped for advice, including Edward Straka, a Riverside resident and architect who had studied under noted landscape architect Alfred Caldwell. Straka, who donated much of his time to help the village, wrote in his 1981 report, "The Riverside landscape has suffered from a great deal of plant loss, especially elms, larches, birches, oaks, cottonwoods, understory trees and shrubs. The most recent intensified loss of elms and the magnitude of its understory tree and shrub loss has weakened the landscape's strength."[6] Straka's recommendations emphasized plant groupings of one type or compatible species, irregular arrangements, and curved borders; an informal, countryside appearance; individual plants subordinated to the whole; and exclusion of unusual or exotic plants or flower beds not compatible with Olmsted's design.

Straka questioned recent reforestation efforts, pointing out they were incompatible with Olmsted's design in that the trees were mostly mature and were sited poorly; "therefore, these trees have interrupted, and in some cases have begun to destroy the landscape's scenic and spacious quality."[7] He noted that the growing body of information about Riverside's heritage could better inform the efforts to rehabilitate the Olmsted landscape design. The Straka report continues as an important reference in Riverside's tree selection and grouping.

In the mid-1980s, a majority of trees in Riverside's small parks remained elms and oaks, and the death knell had already tolled for the elms. The village board approved a plan from the Forest Advisory Commission in 1984 to replant many of the triangular parks in the northwest portion of the village. The tree and shrub ordinance was amended to forbid public parkway planting of the following "weed" trees: white poplar, silver maple, box elder, Siberian elm, black locust, honey locust, ailanthus, cottonwood, or white mulberry. Trees were to be less than two inches in diameter to improve viability.[8] How forestry had advanced since Riverside's earliest planting of giant trees raided from the nearby forests!

Straka's report was augmented by another analysis in 1985 by Malcolm Cairns and Gary Kesler, both landscape architects and university professors. The Cairns-Kesler report, which included a study of the pre-Olmsted landforms of the village topography, concurred with Straka that the contemporary landscape essentially followed Olmsted's ideal of the pastoral, in the residential and triangular park groupings, and of the picturesque, along the river. The increased housing density and concrete curbs detracted from the original design but were acknowledged as a fait accompli. The report included observations and specific suggestions for landscapes:

- Better massing of trees was needed on the Longcommon
- Inappropriate yew plantings were found in Guthrie Park
- Dense shrubbery along Riverside Road limited views to river
- Scrubby weed trees were present along the west bluff near Swan Pond and along the riverbank edge
- Trees were planted in scattered fashion on the riverbank near the dam
- Indian Garden parking areas were unattractive, and recreation areas were undefined
- At the Bloomingbank Road bluff, vehicular traffic noise was quite evident
- Some plantings in triangular parks blocked views[9]

Cairns and Kesler published their findings in *Landscape Architecture Magazine*, prompting rebuttals from Riverside's Forest Advisory Commission and the Olmsted Society. Although the Cairns-Kesler report was largely positive about the state of Riverside's preservation, Riverside dissenters argued against the pastoral-picturesque Olmsted implementation espoused by the authors and disagreed that tree selection had been haphazard. It was but one of many passionate arguments to follow over the next decades about Olmsted's design intent in Riverside.

In 1991, the Forest Advisory Commission was renamed the Landscape Advisory Committee (later renamed Commission), reflecting a new emphasis on the holistic view of the public landscapes, in addition to the singular focus on tree selection.

GOING NATIVE: "MANY CITIZENS STOOD BY THE LITTLE FLOWERS"

Riverside residents not only were awakened to the forest management needs in the village but also, for perhaps the first time,

This nonnative lilac shrub, likely planted in the years before native trees gained popularity, blooms in Guthrie Park near the train station and the Arcade Building. Photo by author.

became noticeably aware of the role of flowers in an Olmsted design. Many environmental changes affected the country in the 1970s. The first Earth Day, in April 1970, preceded the founding of the U.S. Environmental Protection Agency in December of that year. However, as with most new movements, the number of early adopters tended to be few and mostly belonged to specialized knowledge groups outside the circles of conventional homeowners.

In the 1980s and 1990s, interest in the use of native plants permeated national horticultural communities. First scientists, then environmental groups, and then pioneering home gardeners recognized the value of indigenous plants to wildlife. The national Endangered Species Act of 1973 translated to an Illinois version, which by 1977 included plants as well as fauna. Love of indigenous plants was certainly not new. The Wildflower Preservation Society of the 1920s had wholeheartedly espoused a love of natives. But, in addition to protecting natives in natural areas—the focus of earlier movements—this later incarnation of the native plant supporters stressed planting natives in homeowners' gardens.

Across the country, native plant centers and organizations grew. Nationally, the Texas-based Lady Bird Johnson Wildflower Center opened in 1982, and the Wild Ones, begun informally in 1977, incorporated as a national nonprofit in 1990. Established groups renamed themselves to recognize native plants: the North American Native Plant Society acquired its new name in 1999 (previously the Canadian Wildflower Society). Even the venerable New England Wild Flower Society renamed itself in 2019 as the Native Plant Trust.

Closer to Riverside, the Illinois Native Plant Society evolved in 1986 from a small group in southern Illinois. Regional historical landscape architects who had championed midwestern plants were brought out of obscurity. Author and landscape architect Robert E. Grese published *Jens Jensen: Maker of Natural Parks and Gardens*

in 1992, sparking a resurgence in interest in Jensen, a landscape architect who favored indigenous plants. *Chicagoland Gardening* magazine, a regional publication that started in 1995, featured a regular column on native plants.

In Riverside, native plants were appreciated not only for their wildlife benefits but also for a belief that indigenous plants best embodied Olmstedian design ideals. Riverside's Forest Advisory Commission endorsed native plantings throughout the public parks. Comparing the trees planted in the 1970s with the inventory of existing trees in 1985 reveals a marked shift toward native trees. Nearly all of the trees proposed in the 1984 tree planting plan accepted by the village were natives.

Some Riverside residents advocated unilaterally for native plants as crucial to Olmsted's design principles. Olmsted's prohibition of exotic species that clamored for attention in a naturalistic landscape translated to a misunderstanding that he eschewed all nonnative plants. (As noted earlier, among the trees he proposed for Riverside's public spaces were "European elms.") With good motives and great sincerity, but without a definitive blueprint from Olmsted, many Riversiders fell into two philosophical camps: purist native plant lovers and laissez-faire gardeners.

The argument reached a peak on July 4, 1997. Fourth of July celebrations are a Riverside tradition, tracing back to the apocryphal story of a celebration at Bourbon Springs in 1834.[10] There are basically two choices on the Fourth of July: residents either are in the parade or are watching from the sidelines. Essentially, the whole village turns out. The high school band, the swim club, the Little League teams, the various churches, the businesses, the Scouts—any group of two or more follows the grand marshal and blaring firetrucks down Longcommon Road from Big Ball Park to the center of town. It is a slice of small-town Americana that plays across the nation.

That year, some members of the Riverside Village Board of Trustees thought to enliven the downtown with a happy surprise of plantings along the parade route. Just before parade day, on instruction from the board, public works employees planted red, white, and blue petunias. Many people were, indeed, surprised. Mayhem ensued at town hall meetings and in letters to the editor. One resident chained herself to a lamppost to protest the invasion of the exotic flowers.

The petunia kerfuffle hit national news outlets such as the *Washington Post* and *Garden Design* magazine and had front-page treatment in the *Chicago Tribune*. One landscape architect, on the Landscape Advisory Commission and in favor of the plantings, said, "The character of Riverside has changed, even though we've done a tremendous job of preserving it. What Riverside is missing is a clear vision of where we want to go and what we want to preserve."[11] A local preservationist countered, "It sounds like a silly issue, but it's not silly because of the landmark status of the village. We struggled long and hard to get [the preservation] ordinance, and we wanted it to conform to Olmstedian principles."[12]

Arguments over the petunia planting—and the implications for future plantings—occupied several of the board meetings during the next few months. There was talk of censuring the village president and trustee responsible for the plantings. Eventually, cooler heads prevailed, and the Landscape Advisory Commission developed a list of "appropriate plants" for the central business district. Respected theologian Martin E. Marty, then a Riverside resident of thirty-five years, had perhaps the most sensible comment: "I know enough not to express an opinion on this controversy. Culture wars on international and national levels are lethal. On the local level? Anthropologist Bronislaw Malinowski said that aggression, like charity, begins at home. When the village board voted to tear up the petunias, many citizens stood by the little flowers. Civil peace and civility were threatened."[13]

While flower battles and beetles plagued Riverside preservationists on terra firma, the ever-flowing Des Plaines continued to challenge the village. In August 1987, a 100-year flood hit Riverside with a vengeance. Ferocious thunderstorms had pummeled the Chicago region for days. Peaking at 9.9 feet, with a discharge of 9,770 cubic feet per second, the Des Plaines River roared over its banks and deluged low-lying property.[14] Schools let out early, neighbors helped neighbors sandbag to protect homes, and the water streamed down roads and into basements. The flood tested the resilience of the community—even more so because the previous year, another severe flood had brought the river waters to record highs: a 70-year flood event. Other villages along the Des Plaines suffered similarly.

This problem had been years in the making. Increased upstream development over the past decades in the northwest suburbs that had converted wetlands to impermeable surfaces fully taxed the river's capacity. The Flood Disaster Protection Act of 1973 made the purchase of flood insurance mandatory for properties located in Special Flood Hazard Areas of Riverside, thus strongly affecting home values. Many solutions had been studied: in the two decades before the nation's bicentennial, more than twenty interagency plans to address flooding and pollution in the lower Des Plaines River were created by various government and private groups.[15] The Metropolitan Water Reclamation District plan for Chicago's Deep Tunnel, a multi-decade effort to reduce flooding, coincided with the comprehensive Lower Des Plaines Tributaries Watershed Plan, which dates to 1972. Work on the Deep Tunnel, which included blasting at the intersection of First and Forest Avenues, began in August 1989.[16] The watershed plan, involving so many agencies, bobbed and sunk under committee reviews for the better part of the 1970s and early 1980s.

Flooding, resulting from more frequent weather events, can cause nightmares for homeowners. Photo by author.

An early version of a suspension bridge connects Riverside with unincorporated Riverside Lawn. Village of Riverside, Riverside Historical Commission.

Amid all this planning, riverbank communities such as Riverside continued to get wet. Among the many upstream flood prevention proposals, the watershed plan included a dike to be built to safeguard Riverside Lawn. A developer had built this unincorporated community of about forty homes in the early 1900s. Riverside Lawn lies on the floodplain tucked into the bend of the Des Plaines River south of and across the river from Riverside's train depot. It consistently floods during periods of high rainfall.

Riverside historian Herbert Bassman wrote of the flooding threat in Riverside Lawn as an old problem. "This year [1969] they suffered one of the worst flooding conditions in many years primarily because the flood was caused by an ice jam and it occurred during freezing weather. Each time the floods occur basements are inundated and furnace fires are extinguished," he wrote.[17] Bassman recalled different suggestions from the 1940s, ranging

Today's swinging bridge retains its early location but with sturdy steel cables. Photo by William Suriano.

from letting nature take over and build its own dike, to removing the Hofmann Dam and widening and deepening the river. The latter solution ignored the fact that the top of the old wooden Hofmann Dam was lower and yet floods still occurred, according to Bassman.

The proposed Riverside Lawn dike, shaped like a three-dimensional trapezoid, extended about 2,500 feet long and 10 feet wide at the top. Its height ranged from about 4 to 7 feet. The base width of the dike averaged 32 feet, maxing at 52 feet.[18] Sponsors of the dike ensured constituents that the aesthetics of the dike would be acceptable once vegetation grew atop it.

The Olmsted Society disagreed. For fifteen years, the society lobbied against the dike, urging its members to contact legislators. In an impassioned letter to all Riverside residents in August 1987, the society outlined the possible negative effects of the dike, including increased flooding in Swan Pond, increased residential flooding, a higher cost to taxpayers exceeding routine flood damage cost, and removal of 200-year-old oaks in the forest preserve facing the village.[19]

The Riverside Village Board of Trustees unanimously voted against the dike. Neighboring suburban Brookfield, also fearing increased flooding, likewise voted against the dike. The dike was never built.

The river, shared by many communities, required constant monitoring. Often, this pitted one community against another, as in the case of the dike, but more often, communities shared similar issues and sought complementary solutions. In the early 1990s, fourteen municipalities banded together to monitor river gauges and send early warnings of potential floods.[20]

While the dike may have divided Riverside Lawn from Riverside and Brookfield, pollution issues concerned all. In 1971, *Suburban Life* newspaper captured a photo of billowing foam from detergents flowing and bubbling near the Hofmann Dam. "The detergent foam situation on the river acts up every now and then," the article stated.[21] Such pollutants wreaked havoc on the watershed wildlife. In 1976, Northern Illinois Planning Commission staff conducted a biological survey of the Des Plaines River in Cook County and found that only 2 percent of the fifty-five monitoring sites could be classified as "balanced," the best score on a four-point scale. The majority of sites (64 percent) were labeled as "semi-polluted," the second-to-last point on the scale. The Des Plaines at Riverside fell into that semi-polluted category.[22]

In 1978, a petition signed by 356 Riverside residents was sent to the State of Illinois Pollution Control Board asking for improvement of water quality standards. *Suburban Life* reported that pollution prevention rules had not been followed, resulting in "settleable solids, scum, sludge, odorous and odor-producing substances which render the river unfit for recreation use . . . and virtually uninhabitable to all forms of aquatic life other than scavenger fish."[23]

Constant vigilance of the new EPA laws and the positive effect of the Chicago Deep Tunnel project helped improve the river's water quality, such that by the early 1990s, fishing near Riverside's bridges became popular. The *Chicago Tribune*'s outdoor reporter John Husar enjoyed a Riverside sojourn in 1993: "In the three hours beside the Barrypoint Bridge the other day three of us caught 100 bluegill, sunfish and pumpkinseed all thriving in the Des Plaines."[24] Because of Riverside's early history with unwanted visitors fishing, bank fishing was still not permitted. However, avid anglers got around this law by launching canoes and kayaks or wading in the boil of rapids near the river bend. The river started to reclaim its pristine waters as when Olmsted first saw it.

Natural features of Riverside's landscape appealed to many preservationists, but saving landmark structures hit a bit closer to home. While the 1970 landmark status and subsequent 1975 centennial celebration enhanced residents' appreciation of the village's historic treasures, sentiment—not ordinances—protected Riverside's history. Projects that may have an adverse effect on landmark status must be reviewed by state and federal authorities, but legal and punitive actions are not as stringent as some may think. How would Riverside both formally and informally work to enforce the status?

In 1976, the village allocated funds for the Riverside Historical Museum. This quaint museum, housed in a stone building that was formerly part of the waterworks, would eventually store detailed information about every home in Riverside. Further recognizing Riverside's historic buildings, the board in the late 1970s commissioned an architectural firm to study a detailed restoration effort of the village's train station.

In May 1979, the village board designated the boundaries of the village's central business district. Commercial properties had existed in Riverside for decades, although the Olmsted and Vaux design had included only two commercial properties, the Riverside Hotel and the Green Block (later named the Arcade Building) near the train depot. The lack of major planned commercial space distinguishes Riverside from modern planned multi-use developments. The grand boulevard from Riverside to downtown Chicago never materialized, and it was impractical to board a train to shop for daily necessities; thus, a nearby solution was needed. Throughout the years, for everyday needs such as groceries and household items, entrepreneurs built stores near the Arcade Building.

Repurposing an old water tower annex, the Riverside Historical Museum (right) holds archives and photo collections. Photo by William Suriano.

Shops grew in a hodgepodge fashion along the only straight streets in Riverside, Burlington and Quincy Roads, which ran parallel to and next to either side of the railroad. Unlike other Chicago area railroad suburbs, Riverside's storefronts faced away from the train tracks, leaving unsightly delivery back entrances to the view of passing train riders. Originally, the Riverside Improvement Company had used Burlington and Quincy Roads as staging areas for equipment and supplies unloaded from railroad cars. The backsides of commercial buildings remain an eyesore to commuter train passengers today.

The first business, aside from the Riverside Hotel, is said to be that of a market and food store owned by John B. Gage around 1888. Later, a tailor and another food market joined them. The first business north of the train tracks was Charles Osberg's in 1904. Osberg also built a length of stores in the 1920s. Quincy Road, on the south side of the tracks, was developed around the same time.[25]

In 1914, a group of some twenty businessmen gathered to form a "Business Man's Association."[26] The business community expanded from a men's club to an official chamber of commerce. Riverside residents patronized their local shops, but by the 1970s, serious competition arose for Riverside small businesses. William Kowinsky wrote of the competition to small shops nationwide in his 1985 book, *The Malling of America*, and Riverside stores felt its effect. The North Riverside Mall, adjacent to Riverside, opened in 1975. Strip malls along Harlem Avenue proliferated. The local population of Riverside was not sufficient to support most businesses, and the "hidden" location of Riverside's downtown did not attract outside visitors.

Therein lay an inherent conflict between businesses and residents: whether or not, or how many, visitors to Riverside are desirable. More shoppers are good for business, but increased traffic is detrimental to the residential quietude most homeowners desire. The village's Economic Development Commission, created in 1994, focused on ways to attract business to Riverside. It continues to try to balance the needs of the business community with the desires of the residents and the expectations of landmark status.

Sometimes Riversiders were forced to choose between principle and pocketbooks. In the late 1980s, to obtain federal grant money, Riverside would have had to straighten or widen some of the village's signature winding roads. "The Village of Riverside has effectively been stopped from proceeding further on Federal Aid Urban System . . . road improvement program to Longcommon and Barrypoint roads due to the fact that the road widths, curb design and angularity of these roads do not comply with the minimum standards established by the Federal Highway Authority," the local newspaper the *Landmark* explained.[27] Despite a personal appeal from local politicians to U.S. Department of Transportation secretary Sam Skinner, the federal ruling stood, and no funding could be obtained.

Road building, initiated by entities other than the village, also threatened the historic design. In the early 1970s, the State of Illinois proposed extending Thirty-First Street to cut through Riverside from west to east. The Village Board of Trustees wrote a strong resolution rejecting that proposal, and the road never materialized.[28]

Threats to historic public property such as roads had been fairly effectively forestalled; however, the late 1980s and 1990s posed issues with teardowns of private homes and potential overbuilding on small lots. This was the era of the McMansion, with very large homes swallowing up small lots. The density of buildings could be the downfall of Riverside's spacious ambience. Olmsted believed

The business district has expanded from Olmsted's single Arcade Building. Photo by William Suriano

in ample spacing between homes to promote airflow and dissipate miasmic vapors. Congested building belonged to urban areas. A solution to prevent teardowns arrived in 1991 when the village's first historic preservation ordinance passed. The ordinance, first proposed by the Historic Preservation Commission in 1989, sparked by the razing of a home on Herrick Road, emphasized preservation of the character of Riverside, the village's National Historic Landmark designation, the park and road system, historically and architecturally important buildings, and the planting theories of Olmsted in parks. Further, the ordinance proposed to promote community education and pride in rural charm and to enhance property values.[29]

The Schermerhorn house is among many local landmarks. Louis Y. Schermerhorn belonged to the architectural firm with partners William Le Baron Jenney and John Bogart. Photo by author.

Two years later, a robust program for identifying local historic landmarks began. This, too, was not without struggle. The State of Illinois had already identified fifty important buildings in Riverside through its 1972 Illinois Historic Structures Survey. How would a homeowner benefit from placing a home in the program, particularly since the homeowner would then be restricted from making certain alterations to the facade visible to the public? "They had a lot of convincing to do to get people not to be afraid of landmarking their homes," said Lonnie Sacchi, former village trustee.[30] Ultimately, as of this writing, seventy-one structures have become locally landmarked.

NOTES FROM THE PRESERVATION ERA

The close of the twentieth century revealed a Village of Riverside on the verge of another major transformation. A century ago, Riverside had reflected the changes of the Industrial Revolution: suburbia captured a new style of living for Americans, no longer isolated on the farm, no longer crowded in the city. The Riverside of 1899 was sparsely populated, with automobiles, refrigerators, air conditioning, and telephones on the near horizon. The toll had been taken on the environment, but the nascent Progressive movement shifted local sentiment toward preservation of wildflowers and nature.

In the 1980s and 1990s, perhaps in reaction to the Levittowns of the United States, a new movement, ultimately labeled the New Urbanism, began. New Urbanism city planning embraces the goals of walkable blocks and streets, close proximity of housing and shopping, and accessible public spaces.[31] The movement does not necessarily physically separate urban from suburban locations, a difference from Riverside's plan. However, walkability and the inclusion of green-filled public spaces are a hallmark of Olmsted's design. New urbanist designs can include "from scratch" developments such as Seaside, Florida, or infill projects such as the Westlawn Gardens in Milwaukee.

On the eve of the new millennium, Riverside had absorbed and tailored new national environmental laws and had reached compromises on native plantings. Preservation ordinances had been modified to meet Riverside's unique circumstances. The village stood at the precipice of the digital revolution, poised with immersive outdoor experiences to challenge the virtual world.

Wildlife abounds in Riverside, which serves as a conservation corridor among fragmented green spaces in the Chicago area. Here, a coyote pauses on the rail line. Photo by Valerie Jisa.

CHAPTER 7

The New Millennium (2000–Present)

As the December 31, 1999, date approached, one issue consumed global attention: Would the lack of two bytes of computer storage bring down the world's technical infrastructure? The Year 2000, or Y2K, became a computer programmer's nightmare of fixing legacy systems to accommodate the millennium date change. But with no major catastrophe, the calendar flipped to January 1, 2000—apocalypse forestalled. Would the 100-years-plus village of Riverside similarly survive through the next millennium?

Oblivious to the man-made world of bits and bytes, the river continued flowing, the trees growing, the wildlife frolicking in Riverside. The effect of computers, with their ever-increasing capacity and functionality, however, dramatically changed residents' interaction with the nature of Riverside. Terms such as "nature-deficit disorder" became popular nationally in describing children's disconnect with the outdoors and their concurrent fixation on indoor video and computer games. "Plant blindness," a term coined in 1998, reflecting an inability to notice or appreciate plants, appears even more pervasive today.[1]

Internet start-ups—the so-called dot-com explosion—coupled with a housing boom in the early part of the new millennium affected daily life and expectations for the future: home sales were brisk, and the ability to work from home expanded. With more and more computer applications, the need to leave the home for shopping, visiting, or entertainment decreased. Low interest rates encouraged a frenzy of home buying, sometimes putting a family's financial standing at risk.

The economic crisis of 2008 brought home sales to a standstill and curbed excessive spending. Then, at the end of 2019, the COVID-19 pandemic struck, locking down more people in their

During the COVID-19 pandemic, individuals sought solace in passive recreation such as walking and birding. Public spaces for active recreation (such as ball fields) were closed. Photo by author.

homes and discouraging indoor gatherings. Would this translate to a love for more simple activities, a "back to nature" movement? As this chapter is still unfolding, much remains to be seen, yet some positive signs are here.

PLANS FOR DOWNTOWN: "DEVELOPMENT PLAN BURST ALONG WITH THE ECONOMY"

The focus of the new millennium began, curiously, with an emphasis on Riverside's central business district (CBD). Several important buildings had degraded over time, and the whole downtown (all two blocks of it) looked downtrodden. The Arcade Building, the only business building dating to the 1870s, sat virtually vacant in 2003, only to become victim of an unscrupulous developer and, later in 2008, the recession. Another anchor building, occupied for years by locally run Henninger's Pharmacy, remained empty when its owner relocated in the late 1990s. Unlike other nearby suburbs whose downtowns looked fresh and trendy, Riverside's streetscape, with vacancies and worn storefronts, looked dowdy and careworn. It was not a source of local pride and potentially deterred prospective homebuyers as well as new businesses.

After much discussion and debate, in 2005 the village's Planning and Zoning Commission approved a new development to be built on the corner site of the former Henninger's Pharmacy building. Plans for the development—a four-story brick structure with condominiums and street-level retail, to be called the Village Center—required several modifications to comply with village aesthetics. It was the first new building in downtown Riverside for decades.

The Riverside Historical Museum, recognizing the sentimental value of Henninger's Pharmacy, sold bricks of the old building as a fundraiser. The developer offered a matching amount for each brick sold. Preservationists were concerned about the height and mass of the building. Some critics thought the projected four-story structure might dwarf the other 1920s- and 1940s-style two-story brick retail structures. Compromises were reached on the height and shape of the roof.

In that same year, the village worked with a consultant to develop a transit-oriented development plan for downtown. This popular urban planning philosophy emphasized mixed-use developments within walking distance of public transit. Of course, Riverside was initially conceived as a railroad suburb, so the idea was not new. But, with available grant money from Metra, Chicago's rail system, a plan materialized for village board approval.

The transit-oriented development plan initially envisioned as many as 100 multifamily housing units in condominium or townhouses in the CBD area, also potentially as tall as the new Village Center building. Plans included a boutique hotel on the former Youth Center site and encouraged more ties with local tourism powerhouses such as Brookfield Zoo and Oak Park.[2] The plan recommended maximizing the natural features of Riverside by expanding a riverfront trail. To finance the redevelopment, tax increment financing (TIF) districts would be established. Concerns grew over the use of TIF funds, particularly because the TIF area included public green space areas such as Swan Pond, and some worried that developers would overbuild. Ultimately, the TIF failed (and thus so did the transit-oriented development plan) by referendum in April 2007. The *Riverside-Brookfield Landmark* editorialized, "It was, in many ways, the embodiment of the real estate bubble economy. And the so-called transit-oriented development plan burst along with the economy."[3]

Another planning effort began in 2012 for the downtown area, this attempt coordinated with the Chicago Metropolitan Agency for Planning (CMAP). The CMAP initiative aimed to help the 284 municipalities in its region plan for a future of increased regional population and associated quality of life issues. The goals of the initiative applicable to Riverside included these:

- Building on transit-oriented development opportunities
- Collaborative planning and interjurisdictional communication
- Water and natural resource protection and enhancement
- Green infrastructure protection and enhancement
- Water and energy conservation and efficiency
- Open space and trails enhancement[4]

The CMAP document recommended many steps to increase patronage of downtown businesses such as improved wayfaring signage, expedited new business approval processes, better landscaping along the train tracks and in the CBD, "shop local" campaigns, and enhanced recreational use of Swan Pond. An interesting comment appeared in the report's section on preservation: "Throughout the planning process, residents communicated a strong desire to share the historical significance of their community with others and welcome visitors to spend time in the CBD. This willingness was remarked upon as a significant and welcome departure from previous community attitudes."[5] The designation as a National Historic Landmark may have contributed to residents' desire to "show off" the village.

An enhancement to the Burlington Streetscape project was the first major element implemented out of many CMAP suggestions in 2016. Grant money had been obtained, and, after several iterations of the design, sidewalks were upgraded with brick-like pavers and a continuous embedded ribbon of pavers suggesting the river. Raised planters of curved stone walls included a mix of native and nonnative colorful plants. The final design, about the fifth iteration

after community input and village board review, still raised criticisms from some. An outspoken minority questioned the aesthetics, and some felt the process too rushed.[6]

While more visually appealing, the success of the downtown makeover is still undecided. Online shopping, nearby strip malls, and a lack of foot traffic have discouraged many businesses. Several new restaurants have moved into the revamped CBD, yet there are still multiple vacancies. The CBD is not an original element of Olmsted's design, which raises the question: If a new element is introduced to a historic master-planned community, should the preservation rules apply? To streamline the business development process, a new community development manager was hired for the village in 2014. Neither the Landscape Advisory Commission nor the Historic Preservation Commission review business applications any longer, and their purview, by ordinance, excludes the CBD. Although the existing village board is sympathetic to both historic preservation and business progress, might a future board be less so? Given that major Olmsted design elements, such as the train station, Guthrie and Swan Parks, and the Arcade Building, are included in the CMAP definition of the CBD, how will these remain safe from development?

ASHES AND AN ARBORETUM: "THE INSECT IS MOVING A LOT FASTER THAN THE RESEARCH"

Outside the central business district, Dutch elm disease relentlessly stalks the parks and natural areas. And, distressingly, in June 2002, the discovery of the emerald ash borer in Michigan led to quarantine measures in Illinois. Ash trees had been one of the most reliable replacements for elms. Riverside's tree canopy included about 1,100 ashes when the emerald ash borer was first

The entire village, certified as a Level II arboretum in 2015, features a collection of native plantings interspersed with climate-appropriate cultivars. Photo by author.

recognized. As of 2020, only about 300 remain. It was déjà vu all over again in the fight to save trees. The village's approach focused on removal of affected trees as no reliable curative remedy was available. Village forester Mike Collins observed, "The insect is moving a lot faster than the research."[7]

In 2015, the village was certified as a Level II arboretum. This certification, determined by ArbNet, a consortium of arboreta, requires meeting stringent criteria, including curation of tree records, diversity of species, and education. The village specified that its specialized collection focused on native trees. The goals of the Riverside Arboretum are these:

- Preserve and care for the trees in Guthrie Park and throughout the Village of Riverside
- Promote public awareness of the trees in the Village
- Demonstrate tree selection and plantings incorporated into Olmstedian principles, specified for Riverside. To wit:
    - Tree collections will have a strong emphasis on native species
    - Trees will be planted in naturalistic groupings
    - Plantings will be designed to incorporate multi-layered design concepts
- Educate residents and visitors about tree species and the ecological and aesthetic value of trees
- Celebrate trees through events within the Arboretum and in the surrounding community[8]

All of the trees on public property are labeled virtually on a map on the village's website. In Guthrie Park, in the center of the village, the trees are also physically labeled with tags showing common and Latin names. The Landscape Advisory Commission periodically conducts public tours of the arboretum to fulfill the education requirement of the certification. As with the historic landmark designation, the arboretum certification helps bring awareness of the village's assets to residents and visitors alike.

The CMAP report identified Swan Pond, often cited as the "jewel" in Riverside's landscape, as a location that could be developed for more public recreation opportunities. Early pictures of Swan Pond indicate that a small tributary of the Des Plaines River created Picnic Island before the streamlet rejoined the main river. The appearance of Swan Pond changed over the years from the rustic Picnic Island, accessible by a fallen log bridge, to an actual pond frequented by a swan, to the manicured lawn favored in WPA times.

Swan Pond had been regraded by the Army Corps of Engineers as part of a river enhancement project in 2012. Unfortunately, the increased occurrence of flood events (a major flood encompassed parts of the village in 2013) rendered the Swan Pond area unsuitable for sports or entertainment festivals. Not only were floods unpredictable, but the long-lasting wet and muddy conditions hampered regular mowing. Riverside's jewel was getting tarnished.

The Landscape Advisory Commission consulted with an ecological restoration landscape architecture firm to develop a plan for the area of Swan Pond that regularly floods. The plan focused on the most flood-prone area and featured drifts of native plants best suited to alternate periods of drought and intense floods. In the summer of 2017, volunteers joined staff from Riverside's Public Works Department to plant 10,000 seedlings, stapled into the muddy ground to prevent heaving from future floods. By the next year, the experimental planting proved somewhat successful, although about 40 percent of some species did not thrive. The village ordered replacement plantings of those that did well, largely grasses and a few forbs—for example, sweet flag, riverbank sedge, brown fox sedge, hard-stemmed bulrush, and red bulrush.

During 2021, following the initial full pandemic year, a bumper crop of dandelions bloomed in Riverside's green spaces. The Public

Works Department noted significant overtime required to mow the dandelions. As a budget alternative to mowing, the village board voted to stop mowing Swan Pond and let nature take over. Unfortunately, because the river deposits seeds from other plants, including invasives, in the area, a suitable ecological management plan is under trial and error as of this writing.

Sustainable plantings accompany major public works projects of the new millennium. A parking lot in the CBD uses permeable pavers and includes a mix of native and low-maintenance plantings. The repaved commuter parking lot near the train tracks, also of permeable material, drains to a bioswale planted with natives. In 2019, an experimental planting of sedges as ground cover under oaks is being tried as an alternative to mulch. But increasing amounts of herbaceous plantings in public parks tax department and volunteer resources, since no horticulturists are on staff.

Invasive plants are a considerable issue in Riverside's natural landscapes. As with many American public lands, invasive plants crowd out desirable plantings. In its landscape maintenance protocol, the village currently uses herbicide judiciously on public lawns and works with the Frederick Law Olmsted Society and other volunteer groups to tackle buckthorn and other invasives.

The Landscape Advisory Commission, by ordinance, developed a Master Landscape Plan for the village in 2015. Referencing writings by Charles Beveridge, Malcolm Cairns, and others, the document describes the "ideal" state of the design for the commons, playground parks, triangular parks, and natural areas. The commission, working with the village forester, is charged with reviewing the landscape against these guidelines at least every five years.

The dedicated effort on enhancing the natural areas has led to increased interesting wildlife. Today many birders can be seen, binoculars around neck, peering skyward, especially during bird migratory seasons of spring and fall. The trails along the Des Plaines River have been designated an Important Bird Area by the Audubon Society. A Facebook group on Riverside's natural areas is popular.

In another happy success story for green space, the Parks and Recreation Department acquired a new park, not shown on the General Plan of Riverside. This new green space, Patriot's Park, lay in an unused strip of land along the northern village border, Twenty-Sixth Street. Outfitted through grants and donations, it now offers recreational opportunities, plus screening of the busy traffic.

A challenge for the Parks and Recreation Department arose in 2010 through 2013. New village board members proposed reorganizing the autonomous department into an advisory commission, with the goal of constraining the budgets.[9] Since 1937, when the then-named Recreation Board was first established, taxes had been levied specifically for recreation and playground purposes. The economic recession of 2008 strained that budget for the next two years. In 2013, the village board reversed itself and restored the Parks and Recreation Board. Programming continues, with the inevitable controversies over appropriate use of passive and recreational space.

HOME GARDENING IN THE NEW MILLENNIUM: "AN INTERESTING JUXTAPOSITION"

Native plantings surrounding home residences have not garnered as much acceptance as in Riverside's public lands. While some homeowners have adopted small beds of native plants, few have transformed their gardens to predominantly feature natives. Many Riverside front gardens remain traditional, with foundation evergreen plants and manicured grass. Backyards tend to be the

areas where homeowners display their creativity in gardening, and a host of garden styles prevail. In 1870, homeowners may proudly have indicated their available leisure time with a croquet set in the front yard. Today, soccer nets, swimming pools, or even makeshift hockey rinks adorn the backyard. A recent nationwide emphasis on pollinator gardens has resulted in pocket plantings of milkweed and other natives.

Riverside currently displays an interesting juxtaposition of gardening trends. On the one hand, there are more instances of lawn care companies maintaining properties. On many a Thursday morning—which seems to be the day scheduled for most companies—the air resounds with the high-decibel cacophony of "mow and blow" two-stroke gas leaf blowers. Yet, while many homeowners are outsourcing their garden maintenance, others are delving into the so-called homesteading movement. Requests have been made to the village board for permission to raise chickens and bees on home grounds. Other localized social media groups espouse kitchen gardens and homegrown vegetables and fruits. In this respect, gardens have come full circle, with backyard dependencies such as chicken coops reemerging even as online grocery delivery becomes available.

The Riverside Garden Club celebrated its 100th anniversary in 2021. Membership has declined, consistent with national trends in garden clubs. Alternate sources of garden information are available through social media and classes in Chicago area public gardens. But the club still retains stalwart members who maintain the Guthrie Memorial, a historic horse trough now used as a flower planter.

Ironically, in the village created by Olmsted, the "Father of American Landscape Architecture," few home gardens are professionally designed. In 2005, one criterion for selection in the Riverside Garden Club's Garden Walk was that the garden had to have

Birders enjoy migratory seasons and frequent spottings of colorful birds such as these cedar waxwings. Photo by Valerie Jisa.

been designed and maintained by professionals.[10] This changed for the 2011 Garden Walk, where gardens, professionally designed but maintained by homeowners, were featured. It is unclear whether the relative lack of landscape architecture influence on home gardens in Riverside is a benefit or not. More affluent western suburbs, such as Hinsdale and Oak Brook, have a high percentage of professionally designed and beautiful gardens. There is a danger of homogenization with these landscapes, however, perhaps deriving from the commonality of the McMansion architecture. Riverside gardens at their best are quirky.

LATCHKEY AND FREE-RANGE KIDS: "FISHING POLES ACROSS THE HANDLEBARS"

Programs to entertain youth have always been an issue, as they pertain to Riverside public landscapes. Ever since "You can't keep the boy on the farm," parents have struggled with what to do with their children once they hit their teen years. Much of the underlying prompts for "supervised recreation" in the WPA era focused on children, no doubt because more leisure time now filled their days. The juvenile delinquent trope of the 1950s was, perhaps, the impetus that helped build Riverside's Youth Center. With the closing of the Youth Center in 1983, recreation for youth (especially) again took center stage. And, with the constant battles over Riverside's public space as recreation areas, questions continue to surface over appropriate usage of public space.

One example vividly shows how proprietary Riverside homeowners feel about their nearby parks. As a result of the Landscape Advisory Commission's review of the public triangles, one triangle was identified as needing significant work. The park scored low on the evaluation due to the presence of diseased trees and a lack of understory. It was a relatively large triangular park, designated for "active" recreation. Working with a landscape architect, the Frederick Law Olmsted Society offered to purchase plants and trees as needed to help redesign the park. The society invited residents whose homes circled the park to participate in the redesign process.

Neighbors argued passionately about the proposed redesign of the triangle. They pointed out that neighborhood children used the triangle for pickup baseball, and even though the redesign could accommodate the games, the slightest changes were unwelcome. A four-foot dirt path between some shrubs needed to be maintained, for example, because it was most convenient for the kids. One homeowner noted that he had specifically purchased his home because of the proximity to this park. Primarily, however, the project was abandoned because there was no appetite among this group of neighbors to maintain any new plantings on a volunteer basis. The society ultimately worked with another neighborhood group to enhance their nearby triangular park; some gardening aficionados among these neighbors offered to help maintain the plants in their first vulnerable years of growth. This case pointed not only to the perceived importance of parks for children's activities but also to the challenge in obtaining volunteer stewardship of the landscape.

In 2017, the village board made a seemingly obvious but still contested decision to lift the ban on fishing and picnicking in Riverside's natural areas. Those who wanted to lift the long-standing ban argued that Riverside already had ordinances against alcohol and rowdiness in the parks—the underlying causes of the fishing and picnicking restrictions. It is perhaps one of the clearest signs that Riverside is open to visitors and that conditions of the outlying forest preserves and other neighborhood attractions have changed for the better.

Although Riverside youth are as prone as others nationwide to focus on digital entertainments, there is encouraging anecdotal evidence that, as Olmsted hoped, the outdoors appeals to children. It is common to see children riding bikes toward the river with fishing poles across the handlebars. Baseball bats poke out from backpacks as other youths ride or walk to a Little League game. Yet, opportunities for children (and adults) to explore nature in Riverside's backyard, along the river for example, could be expanded. Informally, residents post wildlife sightings on social media groups. The Landscape Advisory Commission hosts occasional tours of Riverside's arboretum, and the Parks and Recreation Department or public library will often sponsor a nature-related program. The Girl Scouts and Boy Scouts also offer outdoors programs.

Riverside children are not, by and large, free-range kids, although informal discussions with parents in other suburbs suggest that Riversiders are more in touch with nature than others. The village is not isolated from crime issues, however, nor do daily headlines about national childhood tragedies inspire parents to allow their children free rein to roam the forests unsupervised.

THE UNDAMMING AND WALL BUILDING

In his preliminary report, Olmsted wrote this about what was then called the Fox Dam, above the bridge linking Lyons and Riverside: "It will probably be best to increase the height of the mill-dam so as to enlarge the area of the water suitable for boating and skating, and so as to completely cover some low, flat ground now exposed in low stages of the river. At the same time, a larger outlet should be provided to prevent floods above the dam from injuring the shore."[11] The stone and timber Fox dam, which replaced an earlier dam built by fur traders David and Barnabas Laughton, powered a gristmill.

Kids enjoy the annual fishing derby or, as shown here, simply fishing with string and hook. Photo by author.

Olmsted envisioned the recreational possibilities of the dam but evidently not the environmental drawbacks. Neither did he then know that several other dams would be built upstream on the Des Plaines River, further degrading habitat and slowing the stream flow. George Hofmann purchased the Fox dam in 1907 and made improvements. In 1936, the WPA removed a failed wooden superstructure on the concrete dam, effectively lowering the crest height of the river.[12] Later, in the 1950s, the State of Illinois rebuilt the horseshoe shape of the dam to a straight-line concrete dam with a higher crest level.

The Illinois Department of Natural Resources began exploring the idea of removing the Hofmann Dam, along with several upstream dams, in the late 1990s. The goal was to increase the environmental quality of the river. A local group, the Hofmann River Rats, fishing hobbyists with membership from neighboring suburbs such as Lyons and Cicero, worked with the Department of Natural Resources to perform fish counts upstream and downstream of the dam.

The Village of Riverside does not own the dam (the bedrock under the river at this point is split between Riverside and Lyons), yet the idea of removing the dam sparked controversy. At first, the Frederick Law Olmsted Society supported the project, but as contradictory data emerged on the dam removal effects, the society urged caution. Town hall meetings unveiled discord among residents. Some residents who lived in the Maplewood section of the village feared that the dam would result in an unsightly riverbed in low-water times. Others in the village hoped that the dam removal would alleviate flooding, although the Army Corps of Engineers and other officials carefully avoided promises of reduced flooding.

The Hofmann Dam, having been in place in some form or other for more than 180 years, was removed in 2012. Among six dams slated for removal along the Des Plaines, the "notching" of the Hofmann Dam followed the recent elimination of more than 1,000 dams nationwide.[13] Measurements of fish life above and below the former dam indicate significant improvement in the river's environment. Calculating the "index of biotic integrity" in fish samples between 1983 and 2013, this figure doubled from a mean of fifteen to thirty along the Des Plaines. Specifically, in Riverside, the number of species of fish increased from seven to thirty, and the total number of fish increased almost fivefold.

An environmental success, the dam removal, as projected, was not a panacea for flooding. On Friday, April 19, 2013, the Des Plaines River crested at 11.42 feet, another record-setting height.[14] Sandbagging throughout Riverside commenced, and some homes in low-lying areas incurred significant damage.

Increasing flood and intense weather events are predicted by climatologists as an effect of climate change. According to one report, Cook County has the largest number of FEMA claims in the country.[15] Riverside Lawn, the area for which a dike had been proposed earlier, frequently suffered from floods, but a later plan for a berm was deemed too expensive. Charged with finding ways to reduce these costs, Cook County in 2015 offered a buyout program for the thirty homes in the floodplain area of Riverside Lawn. Within a year, twenty homeowners had accepted the offer, and the homes were slated for demolition. The area now, except for a few homes remaining, has reverted to forest preserve land. An entire community across the river from Riverside has been dismantled.

A different alternative is underway as of 2020 for the west portion of Riverside (seen on the General Plan as the area marked "Land not belonging to the Company"). The Army Corps of Engineers is in discussion with the village about the Groveland Avenue Levee Project. In the conceptual stage since 2015, the project proposes to extend an existing landscaped berm both horizontally and vertically along Forest Avenue, the western gateway to the village.[16] This area of the village, not originally part of Olmsted's plan, suffers significantly from flooding issues. But the floodwall solution, which would extend across many homeowners' backyards, is objectionable to some for both aesthetic and property value reasons. Other residents, while not directly affected, are concerned about the appearance of a heightened floodwall with floodgates at one of Riverside's main gateways.

Climate change threatens Riverside with more frequent, intense storms. In June 2022, with a single powerful storm, Riverside lost more than 100 trees, and at least 650 were damaged.[17] Each season seems to bring more violent storms with power outages and tree damage. Like other villages and cities in the United States, Riverside has begun looking at ways to create climate resiliency in its infrastructure and landscape. In 2023, the Riverside Village Board of Trustees joined with neighboring communities to study the climate change issue.

The dam is gone, the fish are back, but the waters still rise. In Olmsted's General Plan, no residential lots were located against the riverbank; a wide buffer of green space protected both natural area and domicile alike. Olmsted's plan, more than 150 years old, presciently offered excellent advice to preserve unbuilt green space to heal the earth.

Today, Riverside, just west of Chicago, remains a lively suburb with national impact. Photo by Twenty Seven and a Half photography.

CHAPTER 8

The Next 150 Years

As I write these concluding notes in March 2022, the world has been upended by the COVID-19 pandemic. Two years ago, the Chicago area, including Riverside, was asked to "shelter in place," with the possibility of more draconian measures looming. Local schools were closed during the pandemic, and many stores suffered financially. Riverside restaurants offered pickup or delivery service until indoor dining finally resumed. Face masks are still sometimes worn, and more people are working from home. Outside my home office window now, though, nothing much has changed. The occasional car passes by. People are out walking dogs, riding bicycles, strolling along the sidewalks.

How might Olmsted have considered this pandemic? He, who as secretary for the Sanitary Commission reported thousands of soldier deaths from infectious diseases during the Civil War, understood the need for uncongested space and proper hygiene. Olmsted prescribed nature, in his design for Riverside, as the ultimate tonic. And so, we garden, we walk, we appreciate the river, we mingle—at an appropriate distance to discourage the spread of the virus—among the trees of the commons.

For more than 150 years, Riverside continues to revitalize its residents' souls and bodies. Stewardship of the village, long before its 1970 landmark status, derived from residents' desire to maintain the beauty of Olmsted's design. Yet, Riverside's mix of private and public property, unlike other Olmsted-designed spaces, presents challenges that often pit personal ownership rights against community privileges. Each has been countered with a varying degree of either/and preservationist measures from individual leaders, group champions, resident referenda, village ordinances, or external influences (federal or state regulations or social movements). There has not been a silver bullet that has solved all threats; each seems to demand its own solution.

Every decade has brought its challenges to the very nature of the village, but to date, with some exceptions, the essence of Riverside's design remains. The most significant changes, as described in the previous chapters, include new technologies, surrounding demographics and social trends, and, today, climate change. For communities with planning underway or preservation in mind, consider these ubiquitous challenges below.

TECHNOLOGY

Frederick Law Olmsted championed new technologies throughout his career. His design for Riverside emphasized "artificial improvements" such as gas lighting, the use of improved road rollers, and sanitary drinking water. He explored the use of earth closets as alternatives to privies. Then, as always, he questioned whether the new technology would disrupt the harmony of nature. This, then, seems to be a good way to assess new technologies: How much disturbance will they cause to the natural scenery when measured against alleged benefits?

Automobiles not only changed the speed at which drivers enjoyed Riverside's curving roads but also dramatically altered home and garden design. Refrigerators changed the need for kitchen gardens, and air conditioning rendered front porches unnecessary for cooling breezes. The Internet—and all the associated applications that run on it—has altered everything from shopping patterns to entertainment options. Noise pollution, from blaring gas-powered lawn blowers to rumbling trucks nearby, has not yet been tackled in Riverside.

While these advances might result in more time indoors—and assuredly, in the heat of summer this occurs in Riverside—other societal changes have encouraged more outdoor activity. Olmsted, in his *Preliminary Report*, mentioned particular concerns about women and healthful exercise. Commenting on the rudimentary state of walking paths and sidewalks, he said, "Our country-women and girls, instead of taking more exercise in the open air . . . are far more confined in their habits by the walls of their dwelling . . . mainly because they have been obliged to train and adapt themselves during a large part of the year to an avoidance of the annoyances and fatigue of going out."[1] Advancements in women's societal roles, norms for outdoor exercise, and freedom in less restrictive attire now makes the sight of female joggers and bike riders in Riverside commonplace. No longer would Lucy Porter fear for her reputation while bicycling.

Technology is constantly changing. If, for example, driverless, shared cars become the norm, will our garages become new indoor rooms? Will drone delivery take more trucks off the roads? Will better solutions for tree disease allow Riverside's trees to grow even longer? Riverside, unlike some historic homes or national heritage sites, cannot be preserved in amber, because people live here and will want the latest technological improvement. Can we continue to keep the "nature of the design" protected while adopting the best of technology?

BOUNDARIES

The most obvious difference in the General Plan of Riverside and its current state is that almost the entire portion lying west of the Des Plaines River was never developed. This exposed that half of land to other builders. A design principle that Olmsted frequently employed involved the blurring of boundaries. That is, he manipulated vistas with plantings so as to eliminate or soften any hard margins. Olmsted scholar Charles Beveridge explains, "The boundary was indistinct, due to the 'obscurity of detail further away' produced by the uneven line and intricate foliage of the trees on the edge of the open space."[2]

In 1869, Riverside's perimeter would have been surrounded by prairie or farmland, neither of which would have posed objectionable views. But Olmsted, as evidenced in his writings about New York's Central Park and other cities, certainly planned for the encroachment of growing urban centers. He buffered all of Riverside's borders along the Des Plaines River with belts of trees. The east and north sides he left open to residential development, and he even platted homesites along the current Harlem Avenue and Twenty-Sixth Street. The views from driving along the roads were of either natural areas or residential scenes.

Through years of lobbying by many in the Cook County area, including Riversiders, the "borrowed view" from Riverside's western side, although not as Olmsted designed, is enhanced by forest preserves. This is not the case for, especially, the southern gateway bridge where the Village of Lyons owns land across the river. Five-story condo buildings were erected next to the Hofmann Tower and loom over the river, especially when the riverbank trees lose leaves in fall. Ironically, it was Olmsted's colleague William Le Baron Jenney who made possible the skyscraper in Chicago. Tall, obtrusive buildings may have their place in an urban center but destroy the seemingly infinite horizon Olmsted designed for Riverside.

"We want depth of wood enough about it not only in hot weather, but to completely shut out the city from our landscapes," Olmsted said of designing a landscape.[3] Options exist but are limited for screening out undesirable views from Riverside roads. It is a challenge to identify which trees can be used for effective screening without losing open park space or avoiding a regimented, artificial belt of evergreens. Controlling the aesthetics of one's neighbors is not possible, but finding ways to provide preferable scenery on one's own property is a viable solution.

Overarching federal and state regulations can interfere with the village aesthetics. Road signs, with glaring reflectivity, size, shape, and position, are dictated by the Illinois Department of Transportation. And Americans with Disabilities Act rules govern new construction and major rehabilitation efforts. The village installed bright orange ADA-compliant detectable warning tiles on every sidewalk where it meets the road. While few can object to making roads and sidewalks accessible, sometimes the solution is overengineered without reflecting Riverside's unique character. Roads surrounding Riverside and the river itself are under federal and state jurisdiction. Thus, truck routes, with their attendant noise, surround three sides of Riverside. Only the planting of more trees can muffle the sound.

Riverside has never sought to be a gated community. Even though virtually all of the abundant green space and natural attractions are paid for by local residents through taxes, the village welcomes visitors to enjoy the space. Throughout the village's history, however, there have been instances—such as the fishing ban—when seemingly unfriendly actions needed to be taken. New technologies of today also bring in more traffic: with GPS, outsiders rarely get lost in Riverside's curving streets. This brings an influx of "cut-through" traffic with drivers who wish to avoid the stoplights and congestion of surrounding four-lane roads. Unfortunately, visitors often neglect to see the reduced speed limit signs in Riverside, causing safety issues. GPS mapping is both a boon and a bane: visitors are no longer lost, but speeding cars can readily find shortcuts.

HEALTH AND COMMUNITY

Nature as a tonic has always beguiled Riverside residents. Although some of the outdoor activities that Olmsted espoused—skating on the river comes to mind—are not allowed or popular today, a great deal of outdoor recreation is sponsored by Riverside organizations. Bicycle riding is promoted with signage indicating best routes. Organized 5K footraces trace curving routes in summer and fall. Fishing (now allowed), pickup baseball games, outdoor yoga classes, tennis, and more encourage people to go outside. Perhaps the most enduring is the simplest—a leisurely stroll outdoors.

The promenade of which Olmsted was so enamored, and which he'd hoped would occur along the planned boulevard from Riverside to Chicago, never materialized. Speaking of the promenade in his *Preliminary Report*, Olmsted enthused, "It is an open-air gathering for the purpose of easy, friendly, unceremonious greetings, for the enjoyment of change of scene, of cheerful and exhilarating sights and sounds, and of various good cheer, to which the people of a town, of all classes, harmoniously resort on equal terms, as to a common property."[4] Yet walking and strolling are perhaps one of Riversiders' favorite pastimes. Riversiders like to walk along the river and "just look at the greenery," according to a poll conducted in 2018.[5] This subliminal restorative effect of nature has endured through time.

In 2020, the pandemic swept across the United States and world. In the City of Chicago, the mayor was compelled to close critical green areas such as the Lakefront bicycle and running paths and the popular 606 Trail because individuals congregated, exposing the public to contagion. Other major metropolitan areas were also forced to make these difficult decisions to restrict limited green space. Riverside, so fortuitously blessed with abundant green space, offered residents a sanctuary from the confines of quarantine. Even though Riverside parks were closed to organized sports and large gatherings during the pandemic, residents could simply step outside their homes and enjoy passive recreation amid the 150-year-old trees and greenswards.

CLIMATE CHANGE CHALLENGE

Certainly, climate change is a threat with global implications. Riverside experiences this directly with the increased number of extreme flood events in the past two decades. In 2008, residents were asked in a referendum whether they wanted the village to "initiate and promote environmental best practices and procedures, including encouraging more ecologically sustainable building practices, conserving natural resources through better energy management, recycling and the use of renewable energy technologies and increasing efforts to protect and preserve Riverside's parks, wilderness areas and public facilities."[6] Residents voted 75 percent in the affirmative. Steady progress has been made. In 2012, the village made it easier for homeowners to install solar panels and later hosted a "solar summit" with vendors giving tours of homes with solar panels. Rules on beekeeping and raising chickens have been relaxed. The sewer system, patched and fixed over the past 150 years, has been gradually separated into stormwater and sewage, thus relieving pollution into the Des Plaines. Maintenance of turf in public parks includes tall-height mowing and spot spraying only for dandelions.

Much can be done, with careful consideration to the historic landscape design. Preservation of historic or cultural landscapes is particularly challenging in today's threats of climate change, according to Robert Z. Melnick. Since climate change itself, for example, is still under study, Melnick suggests a flexible approach to cultural landscape preservation, asking, "Does it matter more, in preservation terms, whether a landscape retains an exact tree genus and species or that the spatial and visual characteristics of those trees are maintained?"[7]

The 2005 Millennium Ecosystem Assessment, a United Nations initiative with contributions from more than 2,000 authors and reviewers, frames four ecosystem services as essential to human well-being: supporting services such as soil formation, photosynthesis, and nutrient cycling; provisioning services such as food, water, timber, and fuel; regulating services that affect climate, floods, disease, and water quality; and cultural services that provide recreational, aesthetic, and spiritual benefits. The assessment also identifies several constituents of well-being derived from ecosystem services, including health, good social relations, security, and freedom of choice and action.[8]

In sum, contemporary research on the psychosocial benefits of nature contact in urban settings largely substantiates the intuition of Olmsted over a century ago. While terms such as "ecosystem services" and "green infrastructure" were not part of the nineteenth-century lexicon, Olmsted's writings and built work attest to an early understanding of these concepts.[9] His plans for Boston, Buffalo, and New York City included greenswards and linked parks within and around the cities.[10]

In 1878 Boston, Olmsted was asked to develop a solution for the marsh area around Boston. Rejecting the efforts of previous designers, Olmsted proposed to simultaneously solve the drainage problems and transform Back Bay into a public park by constructing a tidal marsh instead of a concrete basin. In so doing, he pursued early expressions of contemporary environmental restoration, the "process of assisting the recovery of an ecosystem that has been degraded, damaged, or destroyed."[11]

One study suggests that the provisions for healthy communities inspired the design for Chicago parks:

As [physician John] Rauch was busy preparing Public Parks, the suburban village of Riverside, Illinois, was being planned nine miles southwest of Chicago's city center. Impressed by the design, Rauch mentioned Riverside in glowing terms in his report. Enviously he noted that the situation for the development was admirable, being a respectable twenty feet above the river's edge, and thereby ensuring healthful drainage, as was not possible in Chicago. . . . But what attracted the attention of Rauch to Olmsted's work went beyond admiration of the designer's art: the physician and the landscape architect were bonded by a shared vocabulary of health, founded on landscape typology. Rauch had been in correspondence with Olmsted—designer of this country's first public park—regarding the preparation of his second report. Olmsted reviewed the first draft of Public Parks and offered suggestions for improvement. When the three park commissions were established in Chicago, both North Park Commissioner Ezra B. McCagg and Rauch separately contacted Olmsted, inviting his firm to become involved in the parks' design. Eventually, Olmsted and Vaux did produce a design for Chicago's South Park.[12]

But how to maintain this beautiful community of Riverside when there are so many ongoing challenges? In New York's Central Park, Olmsted, subsequently hired as an administrator for the park, was responsible for maintenance. This involved training park police, whom he viewed as custodians of the park welfare rather than as militant officials. Author David Thacher explains, "The work of the park police was best thought of as an extension of design, guided by the project's aims just as much as the construction and landscaping work was. . . . The most significant threats to the park's environment involved a kind of death by a thousand cuts."[13]

Those "thousand cuts" could be the single piece of litter, a planting of petunias instead of unobtrusive greenery, or a man-made monument in the middle of a greenway. But, instead of fines or containment, Olmsted espoused "a policing practice that aimed to instill norms of behavior through persuasion and other strategic interventions in situ, with the threat of traditional court-backed sanctions only lurking in the background."[14] Perhaps this is the best motivation for would-be stewards: persuasion and strategic intervention to ensure that Riverside lives yet another 150 years. Riverside is not an artifact but, in fact, a living work of art.

Notes   ℬ   *Bibliography*   ℬ   *Index*

NOTES

Introduction

1. Although Calvert Vaux was an integral partner in the Olmsted and Vaux firm (and, in fact, may have ignited Olmsted's fame by inviting him to participate in the seminal contest to design New York's Central Park), Olmsted is generally credited with the design of Riverside. It was Olmsted who visited the Riverside site and later conducted tours of same.

2. Beveridge, "Frederick Law Olmsted—His Essential Theory."

3. Illinois Department of Natural Resources website, accessed January 28, 2020, https://www.dnr.illinois.gov/education/Pages/ILPrairies.aspx.

4. Melnick, "Climate Change and Landscape Preservation," 40.

1. Laying the Groundwork

1. Poland, "Unconscious Influence."

2. Rybczynski, *Clearing in the Distance*, loc 64.

3. Olmsted, *Frederick Law Olmsted*, loc 789.

4. Olmsted, *Frederick Law Olmsted*, loc 790.

5. Roper, *FLO*.

6. Olmsted, *Frederick Law Olmsted*, loc 358.

7. According to the federal censuses of 1850 and 1860, John Olmsted's real estate was worth $30,000 in 1850 and had appreciated to $55,000 in 1860. His personal estate approximated $75,000 in 1860 (more than $260 million in 2022 dollars). See Ancestry.com census.

8. Olmsted is generally credited with coining the term "landscape architecture," as opposed to "landscape gardening." This preferred title indicates the holistic nature of gardening and manmade structures (i.e., roads, pathways, sidewalks, and so on). Early newspaper accounts, however, did refer to Andrew Jackson Downing as the "Father of American Landscape Architecture." Only in the 1960s do we see newspaper references to Olmsted with this honorarium.

9. Petri, "Olmsted: The Scientific Farmer on Staten Island."

10. Olmsted, *Frederick Law Olmsted*, loc 972.

11. Olmsted, *Frederick Law Olmsted*, loc 988–991.

12. Roper and Woodward, "Fair Play for Olmsted."

13. Roper, *FLO*, 111.

14. Roper, *FLO*, 128.

15. Kang, "160 Years of Central Park."

16. For a brief description of Riverside road names and possible derivations, see S. Olderr, *Origins of Riverside Street Names*, a pamphlet from 1989 held in the Riverside Public Library.

17. Fishman, *Bourgeois Utopias*, 122.

18. Olmsted, Vaux, and Co., *Preliminary Report upon the Proposed Suburban Village at Riverside, Near Chicago*, 7.

19. Fishman, *Bourgeois Utopias*, 130.

20. Roulier, "Frederick Law Olmsted: Democracy by Design."

21. Roulier, "Frederick Law Olmsted: Democracy by Design."

22. Quoted in Schuyler, *New Urban Landscape*, 93.

23. For more on the influence of the unconscious and Olmsted, see I. Fisher, "Frederick Law Olmsted and the Philosophic Background to the City Planning Movement," 188–202.

24. Bushnell, *Unconscious Influence: A Sermon.* For more on the theory of the unconscious and its impact on Olmsted's design, see I. Fisher, "Frederick Law Olmsted and the Philosophic Background to the City Planning Movement."

25. Poland, "Unconscious Influence," 72.

26. Scheper, "Reformist Vision of Frederick Law Olmsted."

27. Charles-Edward Amory Winslow, 1923, as quoted by Institute of Medicine, *Future of Public Health,* chap. 3.

28. T. Fisher, "Frederick Law Olmsted and the Campaign for Public Health."

29. Olmsted, *Frederick Law Olmsted,* loc 10150. Emphasis added.

30. Schuyler, *New Urban Landscape.*

31. Schuyler, *New Urban Landscape,* 37–41.

32. Schuyler, *New Urban Landscape,* 40.

33. A. J. Downing quoted in Leighton, *American Gardens of the Nineteenth Century,* 139–40.

34. De Vorsey, "Origin and Appreciation of Savannah."

35. Milroy, "'For the Like Uses, as the Moore-Fields.'"

36. Evelev, "Rus-Urban Imaginings."

37. Schuyler, "Parks in Urban America."

38. Fishman, *Bourgeois Utopias.*

39. The Llewellyn Historical Society offers possible attribution for the Ramble design to European landscape gardener Eugene A. Baumann; architect and landscape gardener Howard Daniels, who participated in the Central Park competition; or local gardener James MacGall, who hailed from Bermuda. See "History of Llewellyn Park" on Llewellyn Park website, accessed November 7, 2022, https://www.llewellynpark.com/page/13266~93841/history.

40. Chamberlin, *Chicago and Its Suburbs,* 108.

41. Chamberlin, *Chicago and Its Suburbs,* 415.

42. Maloney, *Chicago Gardens,* 233–86.

43. See the page devoted to Riverside on the website describing the documentary *10 Towns That Changed America* (produced by WTTW Chicago, 2016), https://interactive.wttw.com/ten/towns/riverside.

44. Schuyler, *New Urban Landscape,* 162.

45. Jackson, *Crabgrass Frontier,* loc 1542.

46. Jackson goes on to say that Riverside's curvilinear streets have long been absorbed into Chicago. This is most definitely a mischaracterization. Perhaps Jackson means that Riverside is now surrounded by other built suburbs (no part of it touches Chicago). Jackson, *Crabgrass Frontier,* loc 1574.

2. The Genius of the Plan

1. Although the plan derives from the Olmsted and Vaux partnership, this book, without meaning to take away from Calvert Vaux, focuses on the role of Frederick Law Olmsted. Vaux himself deferred to Olmsted when it came to expertise in landscape design, and it appears that Olmsted was more prominently involved in the Riverside development, offering site tours and working with the developers.

2. Ames and McClelland, *Historic Residential Suburbs,* iii.

3. Olmsted to Riverside Improvement Company, December 28, 1868, Frederick Law Olmsted Papers: Correspondence, 1838–1928, Library of Congress, http://hdl.loc.gov/loc.mss/ms001019.mss35121.0199. In this letter, wherein Olmsted reports on the just-completed topographical survey, Olmsted refers to the 1,600-acre parcel of land.

4. A small portion of Riverside lies to the west of the river. In 2023, it was added to the Landmark district. Other small parcels were acquired on the east side to compose today's current holdings.

5. Olmsted to Mary Olmsted, August 23, 1868, as reprinted in Olmsted, *Years of Olmsted, Vaux & Company*, 268.

6. Olmsted, Vaux, and Co., *Preliminary Report*, 26.

7. Goldthwait, *Physical Features of the Des Plaines Valley*, 84.

8. Goldthwait, *Physical Features of the Des Plaines Valley*, 79.

9. "Overflow of the Desplaines [*sic*] at Riverside and Lyons," *Chicago Tribune*, April 21, 1881, 6.

10. Olmsted, Vaux, and Co., *Preliminary Report*, 17.

11. Olmsted, Vaux, and Co., *Preliminary Report*, 23.

12. Olmsted, Vaux, and Co., *Preliminary Report*, 24.

13. Riverside Village ordinances, 10–9–4: Parkway Landscaping, Village Code of Riverside website, https://codelibrary.amlegal.com /codes/riversideil/latest/riverside_il/0-0-0-1.

14. Olmsted, Vaux, and Co., *Preliminary Report*, 15.

15. Frederick Law Olmsted, undated partial manuscript, in Olmsted, *Years of Olmsted, Vaux & Company*, 303–4.

16. Olmsted, undated partial manuscript, in Olmsted, *Years of Olmsted, Vaux & Company*, 303–4.

17. Beveridge, "Frederick Law Olmsted—His Essential Theory."

18. "The . . . Drives of Chicago: Their Wretched Condition and Neglect. Some Suggestions for Their Improvement," *Chicago Tribune*, September 25, 1863, 4 (ProQuest).

19. "Riverside the Beautiful," *Riverside News*, June 22, 1912, 1. All *Riverside News* citations are from the online collection of Riverside Public Library.

20. "Charter of the New Urbanism."

21. Beveridge, "Olmsted Design Principles: The Seven S's of Olmsted Design." All of Beveridge's quote in this section are from this source.

22. Malcolm Cairns to Cathy Maloney, email, August 31, 2023.

23. Olmsted, Vaux, and Co., *Preliminary Report*, 15.

24. Olmsted, Vaux, and Co., *Preliminary Report*, 28.

25. Unfortunately, Riverside's rules are somewhat vague on this principle. A recent effort is underway that would commingle active and passive recreation by installing a disc golf course in the middle of the public greenway along the river. Wildlife, walkers, joggers, picnickers, birdwatchers, and others who enjoy immersing themselves in the scenery may come in conflict with the golfers.

3. Off the Drawing Boards

1. Olmsted, *Frederick Law Olmsted*, loc 1001.

2. *Prairie Farmer*, July 30, 1864, 2.

3. Keating, *Building Chicago*, 193, restating Homer Hoyt, *One Hundred Years of Land Values in Chicago* (Chicago: University of Chicago Press, 1933), 116. In 1853, the original individual who owned Riverside acreage, Stephen Forbes, sold his property to William B. Egan for twenty dollars an acre. Bassman, *Riverside Then and Now*, 61.

4. *Parks and Property Interests of the City of Chicago*, 19–20.

5. Olmsted to Riverside Improvement Company, December 1, 1868, Frederick Law Olmsted Papers: Correspondence, 1838–1928, Library of Congress, http://hdl.loc.gov/loc.mss/ms001019 .mss35121.0199. In his December letter to the RIC, as yet unincorporated, Olmsted estimated "225,000 feet of lot frontage in your 1600 acres of land and whether the cost of suitable improvements need exceed the rate of $5 per foot of lot frontage." Assuming an average lot frontage of 200 feet, this results in a cost of $1,125,000.

6. Stern and Massengale, *Anglo American Suburb*, 10.

7. William Allen was the youngest at thirty-five and David Gage the oldest at forty-seven. Ages are approximate and based on the federal censuses of 1860 and 1870. See Ancestry.com for censuses.

8. Since before the Civil War, RIC investor William Allen, wholesale grocer of Day, Allen and Co., flourished on Chicago's market mecca, South Water Street. Henry Seelye, a lawyer,

practiced in Chicago since 1850. George Kimbark owned a wholesale hardware concern, led many philanthropic efforts, and outfitted the Kimbark Guards in the Civil War. All of the men had sufficient wealth to diversify their investments into real estate. "Chicago's Moneyed Men," *Detroit Free Press*, May 30, 1869, 4.

9. Pierce, "Riverside, Illinois." There seems to have been some last-minute arm bending to obtain high-profile Chicago-based investors. The RIC bylaws indicate three substitutions for directors: William Allen replaced J. Trumbell Smith, who resigned; George Kimbark substituted for Charles Stanton, also resigned; and A. C. Badger replaced J. L. Brownell, another individual who resigned before the actual incorporation of the RIC.

10. Junkus, "Creative Financing of a Planned Community," 24–27, 36–37. The contract stipulated $20,000 down, $20,000 in three months, and the remaining $260,000 reimbursed from proceeds of lots sold to homeowners.

11. Classified ad 1 (no title), *Chicago Tribune*, May 5, 1869, 1 (ProQuest). In comparison, per Chamberlin's book, *Chicago and Its Suburbs*, in 1868 the Blue Island Land and Building Company, a similar investment group, bought the south suburban undeveloped land, which they renamed Washington Heights, for about $100 per acre (p. 220). Individual investor B. F. Culver bought Lakeview acreage for $1,400 per acre in 1867, but this land was already near the improved area of Lakeview (p. 349). Clyde, the railroad stop on the Chicago, Burlington and Quincy east of Riverside and first platted in 1866, sold tracts for $750 per acre in 1873. Hinsdale, originally laid out in 1866, was improved with a schoolhouse, store, and post office and sold land at $200 to $300 per acre in 1868 (p. 418). Clarendon Hills land sold for about $150 per acre in 1868 (p. 421). Englewood land sold for $1,250 per acre.

12. "Riverside: D.A. Gage Tells the Story of That Suburb," *Chicago Tribune*, July 23, 1874, 4 (ProQuest).

13. Testimony of Emery E. Childs in court cases against Riverside Improvement Company. *Riverside Evidence* (Chicago: Beach, Barnard & Co., 1876), 419.

14. From Emery E. Childs's passport, Ancestry.com.

15. "At Riverside Farm," *Chicago Tribune*, July 5, 1868, 4 (ProQuest).

16. *Parks and Property Interests of the City of Chicago*, 34–35.

17. Olmsted to Mary Olmsted, August 23, 1868, *Years of Olmsted, Vaux & Company*, 266.

18. Olmsted to Calvert Vaux, August 29, 1868, in Olmsted, *Years of Olmsted, Vaux & Company*, 269.

19. Olmsted to Edward Everett Hale, October 21, 1869, in Olmsted, *Years of Olmsted, Vaux & Company*, 346.

20. Olmsted to Edwin Channing Larned, November 10, 1868, in Olmsted, *Years of Olmsted, Vaux & Company*, 291.

21. *Brooklyn Daily Eagle*, October 9, 1868, 3. In October 1868, Childs posted a curious ad in the *Brooklyn Daily Eagle* warning readers of a "young man representing himself to be a brother of mine" who was soliciting loans. Childs asked that L. W. Murray be advised if the imposter was found. Almost a year later, the *Chicago Tribune* reported that Francis R. Childs, secretary of Western Star Metal Company (also presenting himself as secretary of the Riverside Improvement Company), attempted to alter a stock certificate of yet another company to raise $5,000 (*Chicago Tribune*, August 3, 1869, 4). Questions abound on this transaction, since an E. E. Childs was listed in an 1867 Chicago business directory as the vice president of Star Metal with both a Chicago and a Brooklyn office. The 1860 Federal Census shows a Francis R. Childs living in the Gordon Childs household along with a (misspelled) Emery Childs. (See Ancestry.com for census info.) So, whether the real Emery Childs was plagued by a ne'er-do-well sibling, or whether imprudent behavior extended through the family, questions arise. As City of

Chicago treasurer in 1863–64, David Gage was charged but acquitted of using city funds for personal use. At the end of his second term as city treasurer, Gage was charged with defalcation of more than $500,000 in city monies. Until his death in 1889, Gage continued to appeal the verdict while making restitution to the city coffers.

22. "Our Parks: The Proposed Great South and West Side Parks," *Chicago Tribune*, December 6, 1868, 3 (ProQuest).

23. Olmsted to John Olmsted Sr., April 1863, "A Visit to the Army," as reprinted in Olmsted, *Frederick Law Olmsted*, loc 4569–73.

24. Schermerhorn Genealogy and Family Chronicles, Schenectady Digital History Archive, updated 2015, http://www.schenectadyhistory.org/families/schermerhorn/chronicles/4e.html.

25. See "John Bogart" on the Cultural Landscape Foundation website, accessed April 9, 2024, https://tclf.org/pioneer/john-bogart.

26. "Tree-Planting at Riverside," *Chicago Tribune*, February 20, 1870, 4 (ProQuest).

27. "Swindling Subdivisions of Swamp Lands into City Lots," *Chicago Tribune*, February 5, 1871, 2 (ProQuest).

28. *Riverside Gazette*, May 1871.

29. Edgar Sanders, "Riverside," *Prairie Farmer*, May 14, 1870.

30. Maloney, *World's Fair Gardens*, 8–9.

31. "A New Fire Escape and Truck," *Chicago Tribune*, January 29, 1870, https://chipublib.idm.oclc.org/login?url=https://www.proquest.com/historical-newspapers/new-fire-escape-truck/docview/180348637/se-2.

32. Edgar Sanders, *Prairie Farmer*, May 14, 1870.

33. L. Y. Schermerhorn, "Rectilinear vs. Curved Lines for Streets," *Riverside Gazette*, May 1871, 1.

34. Jenney, "Suburban Architecture," *Riverside Gazette*, May 1871, 1.

35. Riverside Improvement Company, *Riverside in 1871*, 13.

36. *Prairie Farmer*, May 20, 1871.

37. "English Sparrow Pest," *Riverside News*, May 6, 1912, 1.

38. Olmsted, Vaux, and Co., *Preliminary Report*, 23.

39. Olmsted to Edward Everett Hale, October 21, 1869, in Frederick Law Olmsted Papers: Correspondence, 1838–1928, Library of Congress, http://hdl.loc.gov/loc.mss/ms001019.mss35121.0199,347.

40. "Riverside Park: A Notable Excursion to the Grounds Yesterday Afternoon," *Chicago Tribune*, May 9, 1869, 3 (ProQuest).

41. Olmsted to Emery E. Childs, October 28, 1869, in Olmsted, *Years of Olmsted, Vaux & Company*, 350.

42. L. Y. Schermerhorn to Olmsted, April 13, 1877, in Frederick Law Olmsted Papers: Correspondence, 1838–1928, Library of Congress, https://www.loc.gov/resource/mss35121.mss35121_016_0188_0271/?sp=64&st=image&r=-0.552,-0.151,2.104,0.932,0.

43. Jackson, *Crabgrass Frontier*, loc 1638.

4. Progressives and Pollution

1. Population figures from Biggest U.S. Cities website, accessed November 12, 2019, https://www.biggestuscities.com/city/chicago-illinois.

2. Walter Nugent, "Demography: Chicago as a Modern World City," in Reiff, Keating, and Grossman, *Encyclopedia of Chicago*, http://www.encyclopedia.chicagohistory.org/pages/962.html.

3. From Ancestry.com death indexes: William T. Allen (1891), David Gage (1889), Leverett Murray (1889), Emery Childs (1886), and George Kimbark (1880).

4. Frederick Law Olmsted, "Village Improvement," *Atlantic Monthly*, June 1905.

5. "The Village of Riverside Fears It Will Lose Its Pleasure Grounds," *Chicago Daily Tribune*, August 19, 1885, 6 (ProQuest).

6. "Village of Riverside Fears It Will Lose Its Pleasure Grounds."

7. Deposition of William Le Baron Jenney by F. F. Reed, in Joshua C. Sanders v. The Village of Riverside, Circuit Court of the U.S. Northern District of Illinois, Case 21878, p. 165, National Archives Building, Chicago.

8. "Colby Gets the Public Parks: Litigation over Land at Riverside Settled," *Chicago Daily Tribune*, August 18, 1894, 13 (ProQuest).

9. Village of Riverside v. Maclean et al., 210 Ill. 308, 71 N.E. 408, 17 (1904).

10. "Progress Made the Last Week: Work Done by the World's Columbian . . . ," *Chicago Daily Tribune*, January 31, 1891, 9 (ProQuest).

11. "Riverside Objects: Villagers Don't Like Cedar Posts for Electric Wires," *Chicago Daily Tribune*, December 20, 1891, https://chipublib.idm.oclc.org/login?url=https://www.proquest.com/historical-newspapers/riverside-objeects/docview/174592794/se-2.

12. From the *Riverside News*: "May Have Electric System," December 9, 1921; "Lighting Problem Given to Village Manager," February 4, 1926; "Evanston Murder Brings Kick Here," August 16, 1928; "Residents Favor Electric Lighting," August 30, 1928; "Compare Lighting Systems," September 6, 1928; "Renewal of Gas Lighting," December 4, 1930.

13. Village of Riverside Ordinance, April 30, 1900, Village of Riverside archives.

14. "Board against Wires Passing over Streets," *Riverside News*, November 6, 1913 (online collection of Riverside Public Library).

15. "Contests and Ties at Riverside: John J. Bryant Elected President of the Village," *Chicago Daily Tribune*, April 22, 1896, 5 (ProQuest).

16. Edmund A. Cummings, "Commuters Push Suburbs West: Pleasant Homes and Fast Transportation Attract City Dwellers. Fine Towns Abound. Truck Gardens and Small Farms Beautify Prospect beyond the Des Plaines," *Chicago Daily Tribune*, June 30, 1912, 1 (ProQuest).

17. "Burlington Shifts Service for the Western Suburbs . . . Abandon Riverside as Terminal," *Chicago Daily Tribune*, June 1, 1912, 13 (ProQuest).

18. "Favor Harlem Avenue Line," *Riverside News*, November 6, 1913 (online collection of Riverside Public Library).

19. Uhlich, "I Left My Heart in Riverside," 32–33.

20. Holt, "No Signs to Mark the Streets; No Numbers on the Houses," 25.

21. "Socialists Vote Down Sympathy. Resolutions Expressing Hope . . . ," *Chicago Daily Tribune*, September 9, 1901, 4 (ProQuest).

22. "Against Boat Landings," *Riverside News*, June 15, 1912, 11.

23. "Sunday Saloons Take New Venue: Heap Declared Prejudiced . . . ," *Chicago Daily Tribune*, March 18, 1908, 3 (ProQuest).

24. "Too Much Lawlessness," *Riverside News*, June 15, 1912, 11.

25. Village of Riverside Ordinance Book Number 9, p. 241, Village of Riverside archives.

26. "Country Club for the Social Workers Dedicated Last Saturday Afternoon," *Riverside News*, June 25, 1917.

27. "Our Wild Flowers," *Riverside News*, April 16, 1914, 11.

28. *Chicago Tribune*, August 25, 1938, 12 (Newspapers.com).

29. Bradley and Perkins, *Report of the Special Park Commission to the City Council of Chicago*, 115.

30. Bradley and Perkins, *Report of Special Park Commission to the City Council of Chicago*, 70.

31. "For a Forest Preserve," *Riverside News*, August 27, 1914.

32. Cook County Forest Preserve website, accessed November 24, 2019, https://fpdcc.com/centennial-history-series-who-put-the-forest-in-the-forest-preserves.

33. "Inspect Outer Park Belt: Legislators and City Officials Tour Proposed . . . ," *Chicago Daily Tribune*, April 27, 1909, 5 (ProQuest); "League Sees Park System: West Side Organization Wants W. S. Control . . . ," *Chicago Daily Tribune*, September 9, 1909, 16 (ProQuest).

34. "Beer in Forest Preserves Recalls Old Time Picnic Groves," *Riverside News*, March 29, 1914.

35. "Too Much Lawlessness," *Riverside News*, June 15, 1912.

36. Cook County Board of Forest Preserve Commissioners, *Forest Preserves of Cook County*, 10.

37. Olmsted, Vaux, and Co., *Preliminary Report*, 15.

38. Egan, *Report of the Sanitary Investigations of the Illinois River and Its Tributaries*, 120.

39. Hannah, *History and Scope of Illinois Drainage Law*, 191.

40. Wisner, *Report on Sewage Disposal*, 14.

41. "Desplaines River Committee Progress Report," *Riverside News*, October 21, 1914. In 1914, Langdon Pearse, an engineer, formed a partnership with Harvard graduate Samuel Greeley, who worked with him at the Sanitary District of Chicago. Their first client was the Sanitary District of Chicago.

42. Chicago Sanitary District, *Report on Pollution of Des Plaines River and Remedies Therefor*, ix.

43. Chicago Sanitary District, *Report on Pollution of Des Plaines River and Remedies Therefor*, 49–53.

44. "Praise Roads of Riverside," *Riverside News*, November 27, 1913, 1.

45. "Joy Riders Arrested," *Riverside News*, July 30, 1914, 1.

46. Seibert, "Concrete Streets at Riverside, Illinois," 12–13.

47. "A Plan to Prevent Auto Accidents," *Riverside News*, February 8, 1923, 1.

48. "Mailmen Ask Relief from Shrub Rains," *Riverside News*, August 22, 1935, 1.

49. Maloney, *World's Fair Gardens*.

50. Anonymous, "Appeal for Pretty Plants," 24.

51. "Fire Destroys Old Landmark: Former Reissig Homestead," *Riverside News*, January 11, 1934.

52. Bassman, *Riverside Then and Now*, 118. Also see Riverside ordinance, "Hospitals Regulate Building Of," January 1, 1901, Village of Riverside archives.

53. *Chicago Examiner*, September 5, 1909.

54. "Garden Beauties May Be Shared with City Unfortunates," *Riverside News*, June 9, 1927, 1.

55. "Dr. Rea Talks to Garden Lovers," *Riverside News*, August 16, 1928, 1.

56. "Time Nears for Flower Planting," *Riverside News*, April 25, 1928, 1.

57. Uhlich, "I Left My Heart in Riverside," 39.

58. Ad in *Riverside News*, May 25, 1912, 1.

59. "Make War on Dandelions," *Riverside News*, May 7, 1914, 1.

60. "Will Beautify Parks," *Riverside News*, April 16, 1914, 1.

61. "Trim Foliage and Shrubbery Appeal," *Riverside News*, August 9, 1928, 1.

62. Bassman, *Riverside Then and Now*, 118.

63. Fogelson, *Bourgeois Nightmares*, 43.

64. Fogelson, *Bourgeois Nightmares*, 77.

65. "Riverside Locks the Stable after the Horse Is Gone," *Chicago Daily Tribune*, May 28, 1922, 25 (ProQuest).

66. "Help Clean Up Vacant Lots Is Plea to Village Residents," *Riverside News*, May 3, 1934, 1.

67. Banks, "Rise of the Municipal Golf Movement."

68. Banks, "Rise of the Municipal Golf Movement."

69. Charles Bartlett, "In the Wake of the News," *Chicago Daily Tribune*, November 30, 1961, 131 (ProQuest).

70. "Protests the Valuation in the Town of Riverside," *Chicago Daily Tribune*, July 14, 1899, 12 (ProQuest).

71. Bassman, *Riverside Then and Now*, 136–37; "Country Club Planned," *Riverside News*, April 16, 1914.

72. Jenkins, *The Lawn*, 48–61.

73. Allyson Hobbs, "Bicycling," in Reiff, Keating, and Grossman, *Encyclopedia of Chicago*, 78, http://www.encyclopedia.chicago history.org/pages/136.html.

74. "Outside the Old Limits," *Chicago Daily Tribune*, July 20, 1890, 31 (ProQuest); "Cycling Notes," *Chicago Daily Tribune*, April 24, 1892, 2 (ProQuest).

75. "Their Wheels Spin: Eight Chicago Women Who Have Made Bicycle 'Centuries,'" *Chicago Daily Tribune*, April 15, 1894, 35 (ProQuest).

76. "Their Wheels Spin," 35.

77. "Club Runs Are Many: Cyclists from All Parts of Chicago Ride to the Suburbs . . . New Bloomer Costumes . . . ," *Chicago Daily Tribune*, April 6, 1896, 8 (ProQuest).

78. "Playing Good Tennis," *Chicago Daily Tribune*, July 13, 1892, 3 (ProQuest).

79. "River Club Is Formed," *Riverside News*, November 28, 1912, 1.

80. Frederick Law Olmsted, "Village Improvement," *Atlantic Monthly*, June 1905. Written by Frederick Law Olmsted Jr. from a manuscript of his father's.

81. Fogelson, *Bourgeois Nightmares*, 124–25.

5. Depression through the Atomic Age

1. Menhinick, "Riverside Sixty Years Later."

2. "Village Healthy Place in Which to Live," *Riverside News*, January 24, 1935, 1.

3. Olmsted, Vaux, and Co., *Preliminary Report*, 14.

4. "War on the Mosquito!," *Chicago Daily Tribune*, July 8, 1914, 3 (ProQuest).

5. W. A. Evans, "Riverside in Mosquito War: Hamlet Plans to Be Ready for Pest," *Chicago Daily Tribune*, July 31, 1914, 7 (ProQuest); W. A. Evans, "Nearby Rivers Mosquito Beds," *Chicago Daily Tribune*, October 3, 1914, 10 (ProQuest).

6. "Mosquito Fight Unabated," *Chicago Daily Tribune*, August 26, 1924, 7 (ProQuest).

7. "Mosquito War Starts to Free Chicago Area," *Chicago Daily Tribune*, January 20, 1926, 5 (ProQuest).

8. "Suburbs $25,000 Fund to Wage War against Mosquitoes," *Chicago Daily Tribune*, May 6, 1927, 31 (ProQuest).

9. Katherine Kelley, "River's Odors Mar Beauties on the Des Plaines: Suburbanites Complain of Pollution," *Chicago Daily Tribune*, September 21, 1930, 7 (ProQuest).

10. "Dig Cut around Dam to Relieve Sewage Menace," *Chicago Daily Tribune*, July 6, 1928, 15 (ProQuest).

11. "Skeeter Plague Called Worst in City's History," *Chicago Daily Tribune*, May 28, 1933, 14 (ProQuest).

12. "Mosquitoes on Job Early; War to Death Opens: Suburbs Are Active in Abatement Work," *Chicago Daily Tribune*, May 10, 1930, 6 (ProQuest).

13. "Protests Halt New Des Plaines River Channel: Riverside Residents Fear Trees Would Suffer," *Chicago Daily Tribune*, September 30, 1934, 1 (ProQuest).

14. "Country Towns Group Supports Mosquito War," *Chicago Daily Tribune*, June 11, 1939, 1 (ProQuest).

15. "Map Battle Mosquito Hordes," *Chicago Daily Tribune*, April 27, 1941, 2 (ProQuest).

16. "DDT to Be Used in Des Plaines Mosquito War," *Chicago Daily Tribune*, April 17, 1946, 23 (ProQuest).

17. "Mosquito Abatement District to Spray Big Area with DDT," *Chicago Daily Tribune*, May 7, 1948, 9 (ProQuest).

18. "Find That DDT Kills Insects, but Not Birds, Forest Preserve Tests Types of Spray," *Chicago Daily Tribune*, December 16, 1949, 4 (ProQuest).

19. Michael Smith, "Mobilize for 1965 Mosquito War," *Chicago Tribune*, May 20, 1965, 1 (ProQuest).

20. Campana, "Dutch Elm Disease as a Municipal Problem in Illinois," 156.

21. "Fight against Dutch Elm Kept Up by Communities," *Chicago Tribune*, December 26, 1963, W2 (ProQuest).

22. U.S. Works Progress Administration and Graham, *Leisure-Time Leadership*, 45.

23. "Movie Made Youth Subject of Lecture," *Riverside News*, April 5, 1934, 1.

24. U.S. Works Progress Administration and Graham, *Leisure-Time Leadership*, 9.

25. "Community Studies Indian Gardens Athletic Field," *Riverside News*, March 29, 1934, 1; "End of CWA Halts Work on Playfield," *Riverside News*, April 5, 1934, 1.

26. "Which Side of the Fence" and "Residents First Division Protest against Playing Field in the Indian Gardens," *Riverside News*, March 22, 1934, 1; "Parks, Safety and Village Clean Up Program in Civics," *Riverside News*, March 8, 1934, 1.

27. Todd, *Chicago Recreation Survey*, 96.

28. "Recreation Project in Village May Be Financed by WPA," *Riverside News*, October 3, 1935, 1.

29. "Riverside Leads in Available Land for Park Purposes," *Riverside News*, February 4, 1937, 1.

30. "Petition Seeks Riverside Vote on Recreation, Proposes New Board and Small Tax," *Chicago Daily Tribune*, February 28, 1937, 1 (ProQuest).

31. Halsey, *Development of Public Recreation in Metropolitan Chicago*, 275.

32. Halsey, *Development of Public Recreation in Metropolitan Chicago*, 276.

33. "Preview of Zoo gives Trade Value to Suburban Area," *Riverside News*, May 17, 1934, 1.

34. "How to Reach New Brookfield Zoo: Directions for Visitors," *Chicago Daily Tribune*, July 1, 1934, 12 (ProQuest). Oddly, the Hollywood train station was not referenced in this map.

35. "Less Zoo Traffic on Village Streets," *Riverside News*, July 29, 1937, 1.

36. "C. G. Sauers Elected President of Assn.," *Riverside News*, January 24, 1935, 1.

37. "Board Formed to Aid Cleaning at Waterways: Seek Return of Beauty, Sports Facilities," *Chicago Daily Tribune*, July 2, 1953, A1 (ProQuest).

38. "Call Hospital, Plating Firm Trouble Spots," *Chicago Daily Tribune*, October 22, 1959, W2 (ProQuest).

39. "Clean Stream Vigilantes Get Assignments," *Chicago Tribune*, April 4, 1963, W2 (ProQuest).

40. "Predict 15,500 in Population in Riverside by 1960," *Riverside News*, July 29, 1937, 1.

41. "Figures Show Village How to Direct Growth," *Riverside News*, July 22, 1937, 1.

42. "Plan Roof Garden Home," *Riverside News*, August 8, 1935.

43. "English Gardens Topic Club Speaker," *Riverside News*, October 31, 1935, 1.

44. "Garden Lovers Club Ends Year, Elects Officers," *Riverside News*, November 19, 1936, 1.

45. "Expect 400 Garden Amateurs at West Suburban Meeting," *Chicago Daily Tribune*, October 17, 1943, W4 (ProQuest).

46. "Garden Club Adds to Village Beauty," *Riverside News*, October 8, 1936, 1.

47. Girling and Helphand, *Yard, Street, Park*.

48. "Riverside Bloc Seeks Defeat of Babson Tax," *Chicago Daily Tribune*, August 19, 1945, W1 (ProQuest).

49. Ernest Fuller, "40 Colonial Units Planned in Riverside: Neglected Style Is Revived," *Chicago Daily Tribune*, June 16, 1956, 1 (ProQuest).

50. Paul, "East Grove of the Oaks," 81. Richard Nickel (1928–72) was a photographer and preservationist in Chicago.

51. Paul, "East Grove of the Oaks," 81.

52. "Frank Lloyd Wright Visits Homes He Designed," *Riverside News*, August 12, 1937, 1.

53. Maloney, *Gardener's Cottage in Riverside*, 37. In 1952, the main estate (bifurcated main home, Gardener's Cottage, stables) was sold to four separate owners. *The Citizen* (Riverside, Ill.), September 12, 1968, 10.

54. Jackson, *Crabgrass Frontier*, loc 5375–76.

55. "Illinois Is the Succor State Colonel Randolph Says," *Riverside News*, January 14, 1937, 1.

56. "Move to Determine if Riverside Is National Landmark," *Chicago Tribune*, February 5, 1970, W3 (ProQuest).

57. As entered in the State Historic Preservation Office, September 15, 1969, HARGIS Reference number 200467, http://gis.hpa .state.il.us/hargis/.

58. Linder, "Let's Go to Horse's Neck," 19.

59. H. W. S. Cleveland to Frederick Law Olmsted, 1889, as quoted by Bluestone, "From Promenade to Park," 529.

60. Jackson, *Crabgrass Frontier*, loc 4528.

6. *Historic Landmark to the New Millennium*

1. Minutes of Forestry Advisory Committee, September 5, 1972, Village of Riverside archives.

2. U.S. Environmental Protection Agency, *Dutch Elm Disease.*

3. Village of Riverside ordinance 1406, August 20, 1979, Village of Riverside archives.

4. "Save the Elms!," *The Landmark*, April 23, 1988, 3. *The Landmark* has undergone several name changes, including the *Riverside-Brookfield Landmark*.

5. Village of Riverside ordinance 1467, August 17, 1981, Village of Riverside archives.

6. Straka, "Riverside Landscape," 5.

7. Straka, "Riverside Landscape," 5.

8. Village of Riverside ordinance 1816, August 15, 1988, Village Code of Riverside website, https://codelibrary.amlegal.com/codes /riversideil/latest/riverside_il/0-0-0-1.

9. Malcolm Cairns and Gary Kesler, *Historic Landscape Evaluation and Conservation Plan*, report to Village of Riverside, 1985, copy in Riverside Public Library.

10. "Long Forgotten 'Bourbon' Site Found in Park," *Suburban Life*, May 25, 1982. Bourbon Springs purportedly represents the site where, in 1837, Daniel Webster arrived from St. Louis and was feted by a Chicago delegation, Jean Baptiste Beaubien was elected as first colonel of the Cook County militia in 1834, and General Winfield Scott and troops camped nearby in 1832. The overgrown plaque, created in the 1935 by the Riverside Garden Club, was rediscovered in 1982.

11. Phuong Le, "Budding Controversy Blooms as Petunia Wars in Riverside," *Chicago Tribune*, April 3, 1998, 1.

12. Le, "Budding Controversy," 1.

13. Marty, "War of the Petunias," 487.

14. Balding and Ishii, "Floods of September 26–October 4, 1986, and August 14–17, 1987 in Illinois," 88.

15. U.S. Environmental Protection Agency, *Summary Report of the Final Environmental Impact Statement*, xvii.

16. "Deep Tunnel Blasting to Begin Aug. 16," *The Landmark*, August 12, 1989, 3.

17. Herbert J. Bassman, "Old Problem: Threat of Flooding," *Riverside Citizen*, February 13, 1969 (Riverside Public Library clippings file).

18. U.S. Soil Conservation Service, "Lower Des Plaines Tributaries Draft Watershed Plan," 114.

19. Letter from the president of the Frederick Law Olmsted Society to "Neighbor," August 5, 1987, author's collection.

20. David Ibata, "14 Towns Take Part in Flood-Watch Plan: Des Plaines River to Be Monitored," *Chicago Tribune*, May 7, 1991, B3 (ProQuest).

21. "From an Unknown Source," *Suburban Life*, May 6, 1971 (Riverside Public Library clippings file).

22. Reilly, "Biological Survey of the Des Plaines River."

23. *Suburban Life* newspaper clipping, November 19, 1978 (Riverside Public Library hanging file LH-690).

24. John Husar, "Des Plaines River in Forefront of Anglers' Surprising Gains," *Chicago Tribune*, May 9, 1993, B12 (ProQuest).

25. "Long List of Business Men Have Served Village," *Riverside News*, October 8, 1936, 1.

26. "Association Is Formed," *Riverside News*, April 16, 1914, 1.

27. "Kubik, Topinka Meet with Skinner on Funding for Road Repairs," *The Landmark*, February 25, 1989, 1.

28. "Oppose State's Highway Plans," *The Citizen* (Riverside, Ill.), February 23, 1972, 1.

29. "Board Hears Preservation Update," *The Landmark*, February 25, 1989, 5; "Board Debates Preservation Ordinance," *The Landmark*, February 11, 1989.

30. "Nancy Foley, 81, One of the Landmark's Founders Promoted Historic Preservation in Riverside," *Riverside-Brookfield Landmark*, December 4, 2012.

31. "What Is New Urbanism?"

7. The New Millennium

1. Allen, *Plant Blindness*, 926; Louv, *Last Child in the Woods*.

2. The Youth Center was closed in 1983.

3. "Seven Years Later, a Gentler Approach to Developing Downtown Riverside," *Riverside-Brookfield Landmark*, March 19, 2013, 3.

4. Chicago Metropolitan Agency for Planning, *Village of Riverside Central Business District Plan*, 2.

5. Chicago Metropolitan Agency for Planning, *Village of Riverside Central Business District Plan*, 49.

6. "Riverside Tweaks Burlington Street Design: Again Concrete Ribbon Gone; Planters Simpler, Lower, Less Geometric," *Riverside-Brookfield Landmark*, December 23, 2014.

7. "Riverside Preparing for Ash Borer Threat," *Riverside-Brookfield Landmark*, August 26, 2008.

8. The author worked with the village forester and the Department of Public Works to obtain certification. These goals were documented in the application for certification, and a description of the arboretum can be seen in the "Village of Riverside, Illinois, Arboretum Plan" section of the *Village of Riverside Master Landscape Plan*, 2015, https://www.riverside.il.us/DocumentCenter/View/5176/Master-Landscape-Plan-2023; and "Village of Riverside," accessed April 11, 2024, ArbNet, http://arbnet.org/morton-register/village-riverside.

9. "Days Numbered for Riverside Rec Board," *Riverside-Brookfield Landmark*, July 20, 2010.

10. "Garden Walk Showcases Riverside's Green Thumbs," *Riverside-Brookfield Landmark*, June 21, 2005.

11. Olmsted, Vaux, and Co., *Preliminary Report*.

12. Frederick Law Olmsted Society website, accessed April 11, 2024, https://www.olmstedsociety.org/education/history-of-dams-in-riverside-il/.

13. Pescitelli, "Undamming the Des Plaines." Technically, the dam was "notched," whereby the main center portion of the dam was removed and the side concrete elements remain.

14. "One for the Record Books," *Riverside-Brookfield Landmark*, April 23, 2013. Although the river gauge measurement methodology changed, this flood was still believed to be a record.

15. "Floodplain Buyout Proposed for Riverside Lawn," *Riverside-Brookfield Landmark*, July 31, 2015.

16. The project was also contemplated in an earlier MWRD study by Christopher B. Burke Engineering Ltd., *Detailed Watershed Plan for the Lower Des Plaines River Watershed*.

17. Bob Uphues, "Riverside Cleanup Cost Tops $680,000 from June Storm," *Riverside Brookfield Landmark*, September 20, 2022.

8. The Next 150 Years

1. Olmsted, Vaux, and Co., *Preliminary Report*, 19.

2. Beveridge, "Frederick Law Olmsted—His Essential Theory."

3. Beveridge and Rocheleau, *Frederick Law Olmsted: Designing the American Landscape*, 80.

4. Olmsted, Vaux, and Co., *Preliminary Report*, 12.

5. The Frederick Law Olmsted Society conducted an online survey in 2018 of Riverside residents to understand their uses of green space. "Looking at greenery" and "walking along the river" at 57 percent and 20 percent of 70 respondent answers topped the five choices. Frederick Law Olmsted Papers, author's collection.

6. "Advisory Referendum Asks Riverside to Go Green," *Riverside-Brookfield Landmark*, July 29, 2008.

7. Melnick, "Deciphering Cultural Landscape Heritage in the Time of Climate Change," 291.

8. Eisenman, "Frederick Law Olmsted, Green Infrastructure, and the Evolving City."

9. Eisenman, "Frederick Law Olmsted, Green Infrastructure, and the Evolving City," 292.

10. Eisenman, "Frederick Law Olmsted, Green Infrastructure, and the Evolving City," 296.

11. Eisenman, "Frederick Law Olmsted, Green Infrastructure, and the Evolving City," 293, 299.

12. Szczygiel and Hewitt, "Nineteenth-Century Medical Landscapes," 728–29.

13. Thacher, "Olmsted's Police," 581.

14. Thacher, "Olmsted's Police," 583.

BIBLIOGRAPHY

Allen, W. 2003. "Plant Blindness." *BioScience* 53 (10): 926. https://doi.org/10.1641/0006-3568(2003)053[0926:PB] 2.0.CO;2.

Ames, D., and L. McClelland. 2002. *Historic Residential Suburbs: Guidelines for Evaluation and Documentation for the National Register of Historic Places.* National Register Bulletin, U.S. Department of the Interior, National Park Service. https://www .nps.gov/subjects/nationalregister/upload/NRB46_Suburbs _part1_508.pdf.

Andreas, A. T. 1884. *History of Cook County, Illinois from the Earliest Period to the Present Time.* Montreal: Bibliothèque nationale du Québec.

Anonymous. 1888. "An Appeal for Pretty Plants." *Garden and Forest* magazine, December 26, 1888.

Balding, G. O., and A. L. Ishii. 1993. "Floods of September 26– October 4, 1986, and August 14–17, 1987, in Illinois." U.S. Geological Survey, Water-Resources Investigations Report 92-4149. https://pubs.usgs.gov/wri/1992/4149/report.pdf.

Banks, A. 1993. "The Rise of the Municipal Golf Movement and Its Influence on Frederick Law Olmsted's Franklin Park." Radcliff Seminars. https://www.nps.gov/articles/000/upload/GOLF-FLO -003-3.pdf.

Bassman, H. J. 1936. *Riverside Then and Now.* Riverside, Ill.: Riverside News.

Beveridge, C. E. 1986. "Olmsted Design Principles: The Seven S's of Olmsted Design." Sherwood Gardens. https://www.sherwood gardens.org/olmsted-design-principles/.

———. 2023. "Frederick Law Olmsted—His Essential Theory." Olmsted Network. https://olmsted.org/frederick-law-olmsted -his-essential-theory/.

Beveridge, C. E., and P. Rocheleau. 1998. *Frederick Law Olmsted: Designing the American Landscape.* New York: Rizzoli.

Bluestone, D. M. 1987. "From Promenade to Park: The Gregarious Origins of Brooklyn's Park Movement." *American Quarterly* 39 (4): 529–50.

Bradley, J. J., and D. H. Perkins. 1905. *Report of the Special Park Commission to the City Council of Chicago on the Subject of a Metropolitan Park System . . . Chicago (Ill.).* Chicago Special Park Commission. Chicago: W. J. Hartman Company.

Bushnell, H. 1852. *Unconscious Influence: A Sermon.* London: Partridge and Oakey. Available through Internet Archive: https://archive.org/details/unconsciousinfloobushgoog/page /n6/mode/2up.

Campana, R. 1958. "Dutch Elm Disease as a Municipal Problem in Illinois." *Illinois Municipal Review,* July 1958. https://www.lib .niu.edu/1958/im5807156.html.

Chamberlin, E. (1874) 1974. *Chicago and Its Suburbs.* Chicago: T. A. Hungerford. Reprint, New York: Arno Press.

"Charter of the New Urbanism." n.d. Congress for the New Urbanism. https://www.cnu.org/who-we-are/charter-new-urbanism.

Chicago Metropolitan Agency for Planning. 2013. *Village of Riverside Central Business District Plan*. https://www.cmap.illinois.gov/documents/10180/24235/Final+Riverside+CBD+Plan+06032013.pdf/045ab947-9e55-4918-b84a-550e7d88351d.

Chicago Sanitary District. 1914. *Report on Pollution of Des Plaines River and Remedies Therefor*. Chicago: Chicago Sanitary District.

Christopher B. Burke Engineering Ltd. 2011. *Detailed Watershed Plan for the Lower Des Plaines River Watershed: Volume 1*. Prepared for the Metropolitan Water Reclamation District. https://legacy.mwrd.org/irj/go/km/docs/documents/MWRD/internet/protecting_the_environment/Stormwater_Management/Pdfs/Lower_Des_Plaines_DWP/Documents/Final_LDPRDWP.pdf.

Cook County Board of Forest Preserve Commissioners. 1918. *The Forest Preserves of Cook County, Owned by the Forest Preserve District of Cook County in the State of Illinois*. Chicago: Clohesey and Co.

de Vorsey, L. 2012. "The Origin and Appreciation of Savannah, Georgia's Historic City Squares." *Southeastern Geographer* 52 (1): 90–99.

Egan, J. A. 1901. *Report of the Sanitary Investigations of the Illinois River and Its Tributaries*. Springfield, Ill.: Phillips Bros.

Eisenman, T. S. 2013. "Frederick Law Olmsted, Green Infrastructure, and the Evolving City." *Journal of Planning History* 12 (4): 287–311. doi: 10.1177/1538513212474227.

Evelev, J. 2014. "Rus-Urban Imaginings: Literature of the American Park Movement and Representations of Social Space in the Mid-Nineteenth Century." *Early American Studies* 12 (1): 174–201.

Fisher, I. 1976. "Frederick Law Olmsted and the Philosophic Background to the City Planning Movement in the United States." PhD diss., Columbia University.

Fisher, T. 2010. "Frederick Law Olmsted and the Campaign for Public Health." *Places Journal*, November 2010. https://doi.org/10.22269/101115.

Fishman, R. 1987. *Bourgeois Utopias: The Rise and Fall of Suburbia*. New York: Basic Books. Kindle ed.

Fogelson, R. M. 2005. *Bourgeois Nightmares: Suburbia, 1870–1930*. New Haven: Yale University Press. Kindle ed.

Girling, C. L., and K. I. Helphand. 1994. *Yard, Street, Park: The Design of Suburban Open Space*. New York: J. Wiley.

Goldthwait, J. W. 1909. *Physical Features of the Des Plaines Valley*. Urbana: University of Illinois.

Halsey, E. 1940. *The Development of Public Recreation In Metropolitan Chicago*. Chicago: Chicago Recreation Commission.

Hannah, H. W. 1960. *History and Scope of Illinois Drainage Law*. An Agricultural Law Research article. The National Agricultural Law Center, University of Arkansas. http://nationalaglawcenter.org/wp-content/uploads/assets/bibarticles/hannah_history.pdf.

Holt, K. 1995. "No Signs to Mark the Streets; No Numbers on the Houses." In *Tell Me a Story: Memories of Riverside*, by Riverside Historical Commission. Riverside, Ill.: Riverside Historical Commission.

Institute of Medicine. 1988. *The Future of Public Health*. Washington, D.C.: National Academies Press. https://www.ncbi.nlm.nih.gov/books/NBK218224/.

Jackson, K. T. 1985. *Crabgrass Frontier: The Suburbanization of the United States*. New York: Oxford University Press. Kindle ed.

Jenkins., V. 1994. *The Lawn: A History of an American Obsession*. Washington, D.C.: Smithsonian Institution Press.

Jenney, W. L. 1871. "Suburban Architecture." *Riverside Gazette*, May 1871.

Junkus, J. 2007. "Creative Financing of a Planned Community: Frederick Law Olmsted and the Riverside Improvement Company." *Financial History* 88:24–27.

Kang, T. 2017. "160 Years of Central Park: A Brief History." Central Park Conservancy. https://www.centralparknyc.org/articles /central-park-history#:~:text=Construction%20began%20on %20the%20Park,and%20all%20built%20by%20hand.

Keating, A. D. 1988. *Building Chicago: Suburban Developers and the Creation of a Divided Metropolis*. Columbus: Ohio State University Press.

Leighton, A. 1987. *American Gardens of the Nineteenth Century: "For Comfort and Affluence."* Amherst: University of Massachusetts Press.

Linder, G. M. 1995. "Let's Go to Horse's Neck." In *Tell Me a Story: Memories of Riverside*, by Riverside Historical Commission. Riverside, Ill.: Riverside Historical Commission.

Louv, R. 2014. *Last Child in the Woods: Saving Our Children from Nature-Deficit Disorder*. Toronto: CNIB.

Maloney, C. J. 2008. *Chicago Gardens: The Early History*. Chicago: University of Chicago Press.

———. 2010. *The Gardener's Cottage in Riverside, Illinois: Living in a Small Masterpiece by Frank Lloyd Wright, Jens Jensen, and Frederick Law Olmsted*. Placitas, N.M.: Center for American Places.

———. 2012. *World's Fair Gardens: Shaping American Landscapes*. Charlottesville: University of Virginia Press.

Marty, M. 1998. "War of the Petunias." *Christian Century*, 115 (14). https://search-ebscohost-com.proxy.lib.miamioh.edu/login .aspx?direct=true&db=ulh&AN=564358&site=eds-live&scope =site.

Melnick, R. Z. 2009. "Climate Change and Landscape Preservation: A Twenty-First-Century Conundrum." *Journal of Preservation Technology*, 40 (3/4): 35–42.

———. 2017. "Deciphering Cultural Landscape Heritage in the Time of Climate Change." *Landscape Journal*, 35 (2): 287–302.

Menhinick, H. K. 1932. "Riverside Sixty Years Later." *Landscape Architecture Magazine*, 22 (2): 109–17. https://www.jstor.org /stable/44660985.

Milroy, E. 2006. "'For the Like Uses, as the Moore-Fields': The Politics of Penn's Squares." *Pennsylvania Magazine of History and Biography* 130 (3): 257–82.

Olmsted, F. L. 1992. *The Years of Olmsted, Vaux & Company, 1865–1874*. Vol. 6 of *The Papers of Frederick Law Olmsted*. Edited by David Schuyler and Jane Turner Censer. Baltimore: Johns Hopkins University Press. Also available through University of Virginia Press website: https://rotunda.upress.virginia.edu /founders/default.xqy?keys=OLMS-print-01-06-02-0008-0003.

———. 2016. *Frederick Law Olmsted: Writings on Landscape, Culture and Society*. Edited by C. E. Beveridge. New York: Library of America. Kindle ed.

Olmsted, F. L., and C. Vaux, and Co. 1868. *Preliminary Report upon the Proposed Suburban Village at Riverside, Near Chicago*. New York: Sutton, Bowne.

The Parks and Property Interests of the City of Chicago: With Maps. 1869. Chicago: Western News Company. https://upload .wikimedia.org/wikipedia/commons/9/9f/The_Parks_and _property_interests_of_the_city_of_Chicago_-_With_maps _%28IA_parkspropertyintoolawr%29.pdf.

Paul, J. 1995. "East Grove of the Oaks." In *Tell Me A Story: Memories of Riverside*, by Riverside Historical Commission, 78–83. Riverside, Ill.: Riverside Historical Commission, 1995.

Pescitelli, S. 2015. "Undamming the Des Plaines." Presentation given March 11, 2015, Riverside Public Library. Frederick Law Olmsted Society. https://www.olmstedsociety.org/events /lectures/lecture-undamming-the-des-plaines/.

Petri, A. 2021. "Olmsted: The Scientific Farmer on Staten Island." Olmsted Network. https://olmsted.org/olmsted-the-scientific -farmer-on-staten-island/.

Pierce, M. A. 2019. "Riverside, Illinois." Documentary History of American Water-works. http://www.waterworkshistory.us/IL /Riverside.

Poland, D. J. 2020."Unconscious Influence: Olmsted's Hartford." Written for the Amistad Committee. State of Connecticut official state website. https://portal.ct.gov/-/media/DECD/Historic -Preservation/03_Technical_Assistance_Research/Research /Frederick-Law-Olmsteds-Hartford2020.pd.

Reiff, J. L., A. D. Keating, and J. R. Grossman, eds. 2005. *Encyclopedia of Chicago*. Chicago: Chicago Historical Society, the Newberry Library, and Northwestern University. http:// encyclopedia.chicagohistory.org/.

Reilly, R. P. 1976. "Biological Survey of the Des Plaines River." Staff Paper No. 7. Chicago: Northeastern Illinois Planning Commission. http://hdl.handle.net/2027/uiug.30112017666311.

Riverside Improvement Company. 1871. *Riverside in 1871: With a Description of Its Improvements: Together with Some Engravings of Views and Buildings*. Chicago: D. and C. H. Blakely.

Roper, L. 1973. *FLO: A Biography of Frederick Law Olmsted*. Baltimore: Johns Hopkins University Press.

Roper, L., and reply by C. Woodward. 1974."Fair Play for Olmsted." *New York Review*, June 13, 1974. https://www.nybooks.com /articles/1974/06/13/fair-play-for-olmsted/.

Roulier, S. 2010."Frederick Law Olmsted: Democracy by Design." *New England Journal of Political Science* 4 (2): 311–43.

Rybczynski, W. 1999. *A Clearing in the Distance: Frederick Law Olmsted and America in the Nineteenth Century*. New York: Simon and Schuster. Kindle ed.

Scheper, G. L. 1989."The Reformist Vision of Frederick Law Olmsted and the Poetics of Park Design." *New England Quarterly* 62 (3): 369–402.

Schuyler, D. 1988. *The New Urban Landscape: The Redefinition of City Form in Nineteenth-Century America*. Baltimore: Johns Hopkins University Press.

———. 2015. "Parks in Urban America." Oxford Research Encyclopedias of American History (online). https://doi.org/10.1093 /acrefore/9780199329175.013.58.

Seibert, F. C. 1920. "Concrete Streets at Riverside, Illinois." *Concrete Highway Magazine*, January 1920, 12–13.

Stern, R. A., and J. M. Massengale, eds. 1981. *The Anglo American Suburb*. London: Architectural Design.

Straka, E. 1981. "The Riverside Landscape: The Understanding, Evaluation, Restoration and Maintenance of the Riverside Landscape." Report written for the Village of Riverside; copy available at the Riverside Public Library.

Szczygiel, B., and R. Hewitt. 2000. "Nineteenth-Century Medical Landscapes: John H. Rauch, Frederick Law Olmsted, and the Search for Salubrity." *Bulletin of the History of Medicine* 74 (4): 708–34. https://www.jstor.org/stable/44444779.

Thacher, D. 2015. "Olmsted's Police." *Law and History Review* 33 (3): 577–620. www.jstor.org/stable/43670798.

Todd, A., ed. 1937. *The Chicago Recreation Survey*. Evanston, Ill.: Chicago Recreation Commission. https://books.google.com /books?id=RYIvAAAAMAAJ.

Uhlich, Robert. 1995. "I Left My Heart in Riverside." In *Tell Me a Story: Memories of Riverside*, by Riverside Historical Commission, 30–41. Riverside, Ill.: Riverside Historical Commission.

U.S. Environmental Protection Agency. 1977. *Summary Report of the Final Environmental Impact Statement (EIS) for the Lower Des Plaines System of the Metropolitan Sanitary District of Greater Chicago's Tunnel and Reservoir Plan*. Chicago: U.S. Environmental Protection Agency Region 5.

———. 1984. *Dutch Elm Disease: Final Report*. Washington, D.C.: U.S. Environmental Protection Agency.

U.S. Soil Conservation Service. 1985. "Lower Des Plaines Tributaries Draft Watershed Plan: Environmental Impact Statement." Northwestern University. https://babel.hathitrust.org/cgi/pt?id =ien.35556030182216&seq=1.

U.S. Works Progress Administration and R. A. Graham. 1938. *Leisure-Time Leadership: WPA Recreation Projects*. Washington, D.C.: U.S. Government Printing Office.

"What Is New Urbanism?" n.d. Congress for the New Urbanism. https://www.cnu.org/resources/what-new-urbanism.

Wisner, G. M. 1911. *Report on Sewage Disposal: The Sanitary District of Chicago*. Chicago Sanitary District, Board of Trustees. Chicago: F. Klein Co.

INDEX

Cathy Jean Maloney is the author of several books on landscape and environmental history. She was formerly senior editor of *Chicagoland Gardening* magazine, and her previous corporate career included twenty-plus years at Accenture. She teaches at the Morton Arboretum, at the Chicago Botanic Garden, and at conferences nationwide.